VINCENZO VENEZIA

misunderstood sons and daughters

A Guide for Parents to Understanding, Accepting, and Loving Your Sons and Daughters for Who They Are and Aspire to Be

© **Copyright 2024 by Vincenzo Venezia - All rights reserved.**

The content contained within this book may not be reproduced, duplicated or transmitted without direct written permission from the author or the publisher.

Under no circumstances will any blame or legal responsibility be held against the publisher, or author, for any damages, reparation, or monetary loss due to the information contained within this book; either directly or indirectly.

Legal Notice:

This book is copyright protected. This book is only for personal use. You cannot amend, distribute, sell, use, quote or paraphrase any part, or the content within this book, without the consent of the author or publisher.

Disclaimer Notice:

Please note the information contained within this document is for educational and entertainment purposes only. All effort has been executed to present accurate, up-to-date, and reliable, complete information. No warranties of any kind are declared or implied. Readers acknowledge that the author is not engaging in the rendering of legal, financial, medical or professional advice.

ASIN: 979-12-81498-63-1

Contents

Introduction	1
Chapter 1: The Roots of Misunderstanding	8
Chapter 2: The Misconception of Parental Expectations	31
Chapter 3: Mindful Parenting	56
Chapter 4: Effective Communication	69
Chapter 5: Recognizing and Improving Parental Mistakes	91
Chapter 6: Prioritizing Your Sons and Daughters	114
Chapter 7: Conflict Resolution Strategies	126
Chapter 8: The Rewards of Understanding and Love	144
Conclusion	156

Introduction

We often forget that we, as parents, were once misunderstood children too. Sometimes we think we know everything about our kids, but the truth is, we don't really know them at all. The cycle of misunderstanding can keep going unless we do something about it. This happens because many parents weren't understood when they were young, and they unknowingly perpetuate this cycle.

Misunderstanding can cause real pain and problems. When parents can't interpret their children's emotional needs, it can lead to feelings of neglect and frustration. These unresolved issues often follow children into adulthood, affecting their self-esteem, relationships, and overall mental health. The longer these misunderstandings persist, the more they can damage the parent-child relationship, sometimes leading to long-term estrangement.

Consider these scenarios, which may feel all too familiar.

You might recall a time when you approached your teenager, sensing something was wrong:

You: *"Hey, you seem quiet. What's going on?"*
Your Teen: *[shrugs] "Nothing."*
You: *"Okay, if you say so. Did you finish your homework?"*
Your Teen: *[annoyed] "Yeah."*
You: *"Good. Make sure you're ready for your test on Friday."*
Your Teen: *[sighs and retreats to their room] "Whatever."*

In this exchange, you might have missed your teen's emotional cues, shifting the focus to school tasks. This left your teen feeling unheard and misunderstood, retreating and feeling even more isolated and frustrated.

Or perhaps this situation with your adult child resonates:

You: *"Hey, you seemed a bit off at the family dinner. Everything okay?"*
Your Adult Child: *[distracted] "Yeah, I'm fine. Just tired."*
You: *"Okay, just checking. By the way, can you help me with the garden this weekend?"*
Your Adult Child: *"Sure."*
You: *"Great. See you then."*

Here, you noticed something was off but quickly moved on to your own needs, missing the chance to connect. Your adult child might have felt brushed off and unsupported, leading to deeper feelings of disconnection and frustration.

We'll explore the often unconscious and sometimes questionable reasons why people have children. Wealthier families, who worry about providing certain services and opportunities, tend to have fewer. There's also a common myth that women mainly want children while men just go along with it. But starting a family just to feel secure isn't the answer.

A big theme of this book is the misunderstanding between parents and their children. Families argue, and children often aren't what parents imagined they'd be. Having kids with the idea they'll take care of you when you're old is a bit selfish. Children didn't ask to be born and shouldn't be saddled with that responsibility.

One mistake parents make is thinking they know their kids inside and out. A mindful parent knows they don't know everything and must learn to understand their children by observing and talking to them. We often stick to boring questions about school or work, forgetting to ask how our children really feel.

This book will guide you to understand your children's true feelings, avoiding judgments based solely on academic or career performance. You'll learn how to really listen to them without imposing unrealistic expectations and how to address their escape into technology, which they often use to avoid reality.

Moreover, this book will help you recognize your own mistakes and improve. You'll learn to be open to dialogue and willing to change for the sake of your children. A parent who accepts their mistakes and seeks to understand them can make a big difference in their children's lives.

You'll also discover how to always make your children a priority, providing them with support and understanding throughout their lives. Being a parent means being there for your children both materially and emotionally, responding with your heart and not just your mind.

This book isn't about blaming or finding a generational culprit. Many of you, now parents, were once children who felt misunderstood and undervalued. As Albert Einstein wisely said, *"Everyone is a genius. But if you judge a fish by its ability to climb a tree, it will live its whole life believing that it is stupid."*

Instead, this book focuses on what you can do now to better understand emotions, communicate effectively, and listen more attentively. It's about building genuine connections with your children. Let's leave blame behind and work towards stronger, more empathetic relationships.

What makes this book unique? Unlike many parenting guides, it helps you truly understand your child's perspective. While it can't replace personalized counseling, it offers practical, jargon-free advice you can use immediately. A full read is recommended to grasp all the concepts.

Think about this: having the tools to read your kids' signals, understand and accept them, and love them the way they need. All children want to be loved, but they need it in their own unique way.

Before we turn the page, let's talk for a moment about what we're going to cover.

We begin by reflecting on our own youth, remembering how misunderstood we felt. This reflection helps us recognize that we don't know everything about our children. Supported by enlightening statistics and studies, we'll see how common these feelings of misunderstanding are and why acknowledging this is the first step to change.

Next, we explore the often unconscious reasons why people have children. Understanding these motivations can shed light on our parenting styles and decisions.

We then tackle the issue of parental expectations. Many parents unknowingly place unrealistic burdens on their children, such as expecting them to care for them in old age. We'll discuss why these expectations are unfair and how they can damage the parent-child relationship.

Moving forward, we focus on truly understanding your child. This involves mindful parenting—observing and talking to your kids beyond surface-level questions. It's about valuing their true feelings and creating a safe space for them to express themselves.

Communication is a cornerstone of this journey. You'll learn how to really listen to your children, avoiding judgments based on their achievements and encouraging open dialogue. These techniques help build trust and understanding.

In our tech-driven world, it's essential to address technological escapism. We'll explore why children turn to screens and how you can help them find balance, fostering real-life connections that are crucial for their development.

Every parent makes mistakes, but recognizing and improving on these mistakes is vital. We'll discuss common parenting pitfalls and how growth and learning from these errors can strengthen your bond with your children.

Prioritizing your children is more than just providing for them materially; it's about emotional support too. We'll cover how to make them feel valued and understood, offering consistent support throughout their lives.

Finally, we celebrate the rewards of understanding and love. Building a relationship based on mutual respect leads to lasting benefits, enriching both your life and your children's. This journey isn't always easy, but the rewards—a stronger, deeper connection—are immeasurable.

Chapter 1: The Roots of Misunderstanding

Let's take a trip down memory lane. Remember being a young person? It wasn't all about fun and freedom; it was a time of intense emotions, confusion, and often feeling misunderstood. You might recall sitting in your room, blasting music, convinced your parents just didn't get you. Now, as parents, the tables have turned.

Reflecting on Past Experiences

Think back to specific instances when you felt deeply misunderstood by your parents. Maybe it was when you wanted to hang out with friends instead of studying for that math test, or when you expressed a passion for a career they didn't approve of. How did their reaction make you feel? Frustrated? Isolated?

Angry? It's likely your children are feeling something similar now.

Take a moment to really immerse yourself in that memory. Close your eyes and try to remember the details. Where were you? What did your parents say? How did you react? Most importantly, how did their reaction make you feel? The point of this exercise isn't to dredge up old feelings but to help you empathize with your children. If we can remember our own struggles with feeling misunderstood, it becomes easier to recognize those same struggles in our children.

Exercise: Reflecting on Your Own Youth

Grab a notebook or open a new document on your computer. Let's do a quick exercise to reflect on your past experiences. Write down your thoughts as you go through the following steps:

1. **Recall a Specific Instance**:

    - Think back to a time in your teenage years when you felt misunderstood by your parents.

    - Write down the situation in detail. What was happening? What did you want or need at that moment?

2. **Describe Your Parents' Reaction**:

    - Write about how your parents reacted to the situation.

    - What did they say or do that made you feel misunderstood?

3. **Identify Your Emotions**:

    - Focus on how their reaction made you feel. Were you frustrated, isolated, angry, or something else?

    - Write a few sentences about your emotions and why you felt that way.

4. **Reflect on the Impact**:

    - Think about how this instance affected your relationship with your parents.

    - Did it lead to more misunderstandings? How did it shape your view of your parents?

5. **Connect to Your Present Experience**:

    - Now, consider how your own children might feel when they perceive being misunderstood by you.

    - Write a few sentences about how your past experience can help you empathize with your children's feelings.

Here's an example to get you started:

Recall a Specific Instance:
"I remember when I was 16 and wanted to join the school band. My parents thought it was a waste of time and insisted I focus on my studies."

Describe Your Parents' Reaction:
"They told me I was being irresponsible and that music wouldn't get me anywhere in life. They refused to let me attend band practice."

Identify Your Emotions:
"I felt crushed and angry. Music was my passion, and their dismissal of it made me feel like they didn't care about what was important to me."

Reflect on the Impact:
"This incident made me feel distant from my parents. I stopped sharing my interests with them because I feared they would judge or reject them."

Connect to Your Present Experience:
"Remembering this, I realize how my own children might feel when I dismiss their interests. It helps me understand the im-

portance of supporting their passions, even if I don't fully understand them."

Taking the time to reflect on your own experiences can provide valuable insights into your children's emotions. By connecting with your past, you can empathize with your children's present struggles, paving the way for better understanding and communication.

Have you done the exercise? Yes, I know you're probably hating me for reminding you of something that was better left relegated to the basement of your mind. Maybe you're thinking, "Yes, it happened to me when I was younger, but it's not the same thing with my child." I'm sorry to tell you, but it is just the same thing. They feel exactly the same as you did years ago. The context and circumstances might be different, but the emotions are unchanged.

P.S.: (Just joking!) There is still time for you to silently close this book and put it back on your bookshelf. But seriously, keep reading to better understand your kids.

Identifying Repeated Patterns

Reflecting on your youth, let's delve deeper. Are the misunderstandings you had with your parents being repeated with your children? This reflection can break cycles and foster healthier communication.

Think of a recent disconnect with your child. Maybe they wanted to hang out with friends when you thought they should study. How did you react? Did you dismiss their feelings, prioritizing your own? Compare this to your teenage years. Did your parents dismiss your interests, seeing them as distractions? Consider the emotions involved. When your parents dismissed your interests, you likely felt frustrated, isolated, or angry. These feelings shape your relationship with them. Now, think about your child's perspective. How might your reaction make them feel? Are they experiencing the same frustration and isolation you once felt?

Identifying these patterns is crucial. If your reactions mirror your parents', you might be repeating cycles of misunderstanding. This isn't about blame; it's about recognizing how your past influences your present behavior.

Imagine your teenage self standing next to your child. Both of you express an important desire, met with a dismissive reaction from a parent. The feelings of being unheard and undervalued are strikingly similar, despite different circumstances. This visualization helps you empathize with your child's experience. Picture the frustration, isolation, and longing for understanding you felt, and see those emotions mirrored in your child's eyes.

This exercise bridges empathy from your past to your child's present, showing that core emotions transcend generations.

Breaking these cycles involves conscious effort and empathy. Next time a similar situation arises, pause and reflect. Instead of dismissing your child's desires, listen. Ask why it's important to them and try to understand their perspective. You don't have to agree with everything, but valuing their feelings can make a significant difference. For instance, if your child wants to spend the weekend with friends but you're concerned about their test, find a middle ground. They can spend time with friends and set aside specific hours for studying. This approach respects their need for social interaction while emphasizing academic responsibilities.

Now, consider an adult child. Perhaps your adult child is contemplating a career change that you see as risky. Instead of dismissing their ambitions, recall a time when your parents doubted your choices. Engage in a conversation about their aspirations and concerns. Offering support rather than judgment can strengthen your relationship and help them feel understood.

Remember, the goal is to be a mindful parent, not a perfect one. Recognizing and addressing these patterns creates a supportive and understanding environment for your children, strengthening your relationship and helping them feel valued and understood.

Recognizing That We Don't Know Everything About Our Sons and Daughters

Let's face it: we don't know everything about our kids. As parents, it's easy to think we have them all figured out. After all, we've known them since they were born. But teenagers and adult children are complex individuals with their own thoughts, feelings, and experiences that we might not fully understand.

Beyond Surface-Level Conversations

Think about the last time you tried to engage in a conversation with your child. Was it focused on surface-level topics like grades or chores? Or did you delve into deeper subjects, such as their dreams, fears, and passions? If your conversations tend to be more about logistics than emotions, you're not alone. Many parents find it challenging to transition from managing their children's day-to-day activities to truly understanding their inner worlds.

This difficulty often stems from a natural shift in the parent-child relationship as children grow. When they are young, parents are primarily caretakers, ensuring their children are safe, healthy, and educated. As children enter their teenage years and beyond, the need for emotional connection and understanding becomes more critical.

Exploring Identities and Facing Barriers

Children and teenagers, in particular, are in a phase of life where they are exploring their identities, forming their own opinions, and developing personal values. This exploration can lead them to experience a wide range of emotions and thoughts that they may not readily share with their parents. They might fear judgment or misunderstanding, or simply feel that their parents won't grasp what they're going through.

Moreover, the generational gap can create additional barriers to understanding. The world that teenagers and young adults navigate today is vastly different from what their parents experienced at the same age. Issues like social media, mental health awareness, and the pressure to succeed academically and professionally are much more prominent now. This disparity can make it even harder for parents to relate to their children's experiences.

Overcoming Preconceived Notions

Parents might also have preconceived notions about their children's interests and capabilities, based on their own dreams or societal expectations. These assumptions can inadvertently stifle a child's ability to express their true selves. For instance, a parent who values academic achievement above all might overlook their child's passion for art or sports, leading the child to feel misunderstood and undervalued.

Recognizing the Evolution of Emotional Needs

As children move from adolescence to adulthood, their emotional needs evolve significantly.

Adolescence: During adolescence, children begin to seek greater independence, exploring their identity, forming their own opinions, and developing personal values. This period of self-discovery often involves testing limits and seeking autonomy, which can create friction in the parent-child relationship. It is critical that parents recognize that this desire for independence is a healthy and necessary part of growing up.

Young Adulthood: Adolescents and young adults often desire validation and understanding from their parents. They want their thoughts, feelings, and experiences to be acknowledged and respected. This need for emotional connection becomes deeper when dealing with the complexities of modern life, including social pressures, academic challenges, and mental health issues. The generation gap can exacerbate these challenges, as parents may have difficulty relating to the very different world their children are experiencing.

Adulthood: As they become adults, children's needs for communication and understanding evolve further. They seek relationships with parents based more on mutual respect and less on authority. Adult children often want to be considered equals, with their own valid perspectives and life experiences. They may make important life decisions, such as career changes, relationships, or starting their own families. At these times, they appreciate parental support that is empathetic and nonjudgmental, rather than prescriptive or dismissive.

Individual Differences

It is also important to consider that each child is unique, with their own experiences and perspectives. Even within the same family, siblings may have very different personalities, interests, and needs. What works for one child in terms of communication and connection may not work for another. Recognizing and respecting these differences is critical to fostering a supportive and understanding relationship with each child.

Adapting Communication Approaches

Parents must try to adapt their approach to communication as their children grow. This involves shifting from a role of direct supervision and control to one of guidance and support. Engaging in open and honest conversations about children's dreams, fears, and aspirations can help bridge the gap created by generational differences. By actively listening and showing genuine interest, parents can create a safe space in which children can express themselves (we will see later how to do it).

Statistics and Studies on Feeling Misunderstood

Feeling disconnected from your child is a common issue, as research reveals many teenagers and adult children often feel they are not understood by their parents. Studies indicate that a notable 60% of teenagers feel their emotional and personal complexities are not grasped by their parents. Such misunderstandings can contribute to several problems such as anxiety, depression, and difficulties in family dynamics.

Furthermore, investigations into family relationships suggest that adult children who continue to feel misunderstood by their parents report decreased satisfaction and closeness in these relationships. The effects of being misunderstood during teenage years can persist into adulthood, potentially undermining the strength of long-term familial bonds. The implications of these strained relationships can significantly affect the emotional health of both parents and their children, impacting the well-being across generations.

Common Signs and Symptoms of an Adversarial Relationship

Recognizing the signs of an adversarial relationship between parents and children is crucial for addressing and mending these bonds. Here are some common symptoms:

For Teenagers:

- Increased Secrecy: Teenagers may become more secretive, hiding aspects of their lives from their parents.

- Frequent Arguments: Disagreements and conflicts become more common, often escalating over minor issues.

- Withdrawal from Family Activities: Teens might distance themselves from family gatherings and prefer solitude or time with friends.

- Decline in Academic Performance: Stress and emotional turmoil can negatively affect their schoolwork and motivation.

- Signs of Anxiety or Depression: Look for changes in mood, sleep patterns, and overall behavior that indicate mental health struggles.

- Rebellious Behavior: Engaging in risky behaviors or breaking rules as a form of expressing frustration or seeking attention.

For Adult Children:

- Minimal Communication: Adult children may reduce the frequency and depth of conversations with their parents.

- Avoidance of Family Events: They might find excuses to skip family gatherings or maintain physical and emotional distance.

- Reluctance to Share Personal Information: Keeping their personal lives private to avoid judgment or criticism.

- Resentment or Bitterness: Harboring unresolved feelings from past conflicts, which can surface during interactions.

- Lack of Emotional Support: Feeling unsupported or misunderstood in their personal choices and struggles.

- Diminished Closeness: A noticeable lack of warmth or connection in the parent-child relationship.

These signs indicate a strained relationship that can have lasting effects on both the parent and the child. Addressing these symptoms early can help in rebuilding trust and fostering a healthier, more supportive dynamic.

Understanding these symptoms is the first step toward mending the relationship. Recognizing the patterns of behavior in both teenagers and adult children can help parents take proactive steps to bridge the emotional gap and create a more understanding and supportive environment.

Unconscious Motivations for Having Children

We've come almost to the end of this chapter, but before we wrap up, let's delve into the reasons why you decided to have children. What are the most common motivations, both conscious and unconscious, that drive people to make this life-changing choice?

Reasons Parents Choose to Have Children

Why do we decide to have children? The reasons are as diverse as they are complex, blending both conscious desires and unconscious drives. For many, having children feels like a natural next step in life, a milestone that brings a sense of purpose and completeness. It's almost as if it's woven into the fabric of our life goals. We grow up with the idea that parenthood is a key part of adulthood, a notion reinforced by cultural and societal expectations. Everywhere we look, there are cues that nudge us toward starting a family, from media portrayals to the traditions passed down through generations.

There's also a powerful desire for legacy. The thought of leaving a part of ourselves behind through our children can be incredibly motivating. It's not just about genetics, but also about passing on family traditions, values, and the essence of who we are. The emotional bonds and joys that children bring into our lives are another significant factor. The love, companionship, and the nurturing experience can be deeply fulfilling, creating an emotional richness that many parents treasure.

For some, the decision to have children is tied to their own past. They see it as an opportunity to heal or relive their childhood experiences, but this time, doing it differently. They hope to create a better version of the family life they once knew, fixing the mistakes of the past and fostering a healthier environment for their own children.

However, it's crucial to acknowledge that not all reasons are driven by such altruistic or thoughtful motivations. In some cases, the decision to have children can stem from more selfish desires—perhaps out of boredom, the illusion of advancing one's life status, or even the fear of loneliness in old age, hoping to have someone who will take care of us later in life. These motivations, while human, point to a more complex and sometimes less noble facet of why we choose to become parents. It raises important questions about the responsibilities and the depth of consideration we owe not only to ourselves but to the potential lives we choose to bring into this world.

Consider this: have you ever deeply thought about why you chose to have children? It's a deeply personal question, but taking a moment to reflect on your own motivations can be enlightening. Was it the desire to build a family and create new memories? Or perhaps it was influenced by your upbringing and the values instilled in you? Maybe it was an innate feeling, a calling that parenthood was your path. Or could it have been influenced by less examined, perhaps more selfish reasons? Reflecting on these motivations isn't about casting judgment but about understanding the complex layers that influence our decisions, which can help us become more mindful and intentional parents.

The Role of Socioeconomic Status in Family Size

Let's talk about how money, education, and careers shape the decisions we make about having kids. Socioeconomic status (SES) is a big player here. Families with more financial stability often find the idea of having children less daunting. When you're not constantly worrying about money, the prospect of adding a little one (or a few) to your household doesn't seem quite as overwhelming. Financial stability means better access to resources, education, healthcare, and all the other essentials that support a larger family.

Think about it: educated parents often have different priorities and expectations when it comes to family planning. They might plan meticulously, balancing career goals with family life. On the flip side, families with lower SES might lean more on extended family and community support, which can influence their decisions on how many kids to have and when to have them. Access to healthcare is another significant factor. Those with higher SES often have better access to family planning services, giving them more control over when and how they grow their families.

Gender Perspectives on Parenthood

Now, let's dive into the whole gender thing because, historically, it's been a game-changer in how we approach parenthood. Women have traditionally faced more societal pressure to become mothers. It's like there's this invisible checklist that says, "Get a job, get married, have kids." This pressure can create deep emotional and psychological expectations around motherhood, making it seem like an obligatory part of being a woman.

On the other hand, men have been seen as the providers, the ones who need to ensure financial stability before starting a family. But guess what? Times are changing, and so are these old-school norms. More and more, we're seeing dads dive into parenting with the same enthusiasm and dedication as moms. Active fatherhood is on the rise, and it's fantastic to see men stepping up and embracing their roles as nurturers and caregivers.

Balancing these roles can be tricky, though. Women often juggle career ambitions and family due to societal expectations, feeling the strain of trying to "do it all." Meanwhile, men who want to be more involved at home might struggle against the breadwinner stereotype. But here's the good news: these roles are becoming more fluid. Society is slowly but surely evolving, and with it, the rigid definitions of what it means to be a mom or a dad are loosening up.

Your Personal Reflection

As we wrap up, we return to why you chose to have children. Reflecting on your own motivations can provide valuable insights into your parenting style and how you relate to your children. Reflecting on your own motivations can provide valuable insights into your parenting style and how you relate to your children. Grab a notebook or open a new document on your computer, and take some time to ponder and write down your thoughts. Here are some questions to guide you:

1. **What were your deepest motivations for becoming a parent?** Reflect on whether these motivations were conscious decisions or if they stemmed from deeper, perhaps unconscious, desires. Did you always envision yourself as a parent, or was there a specific moment or influence that solidified your decision?

2. **How did your own upbringing and the values instilled in you influence your decision to have children?** Think about the family environment you grew up in. Were there specific traditions, beliefs, or experiences that shaped your views on parenthood?

3. **What role did societal or cultural expectations play in your choice to start a family?** Consider how external pressures and cultural norms may have influenced your decision. Did you feel a societal expectation to have children, or was it more of a personal desire?

4. **How do you envision shaping your children's lives and what legacy do you wish to leave through them?** Think about the values, traditions, and lessons you want to pass on. What impact do you hope to have on your children's futures, and how do you want them

to remember you?

5. **How has your financial situation and career aspirations influenced your decisions about family size and timing?** Reflect on how your socioeconomic status has impacted your family planning. Did financial stability make the decision easier, or did career goals and ambitions play a significant role?

6. **How do you and your partner share parenting responsibilities, and how can you embrace more fluid roles?** Consider the current dynamics in your household. Are responsibilities equally shared, or do traditional roles dominate? How can you both become more flexible in your parenting roles to better support each other and your children?

By reflecting on these questions, you might uncover deeper insights into your motivations and how they influence your parenting. Understanding your reasons can help you become more empathetic and intentional in your parenting journey, breaking cycles of misunderstanding and fostering stronger, healthier relationships with your children.

Highlights of The Chapter

In this chapter, we take a heartfelt look at the ups and downs of parent-child relationships by reflecting on our own teenage years. We explore those times when we felt misunderstood by our parents and how those experiences shape our reactions now that we're the ones in charge. Through some thoughtful exercises and relatable stories, we highlight the importance of empathy, recognizing familiar patterns, and breaking cycles of misunderstanding. We also touch on how kids' emotional needs change as they grow, the often unconscious reasons we chose to become parents, and how our financial situation and gender roles influence how we parent.

Key Points to Take Away

- **Remembering Our Teen Years**: Thinking back to when we were teenagers and felt misunderstood can help us relate to what our kids are going through.

- **Self-Reflection Exercise**: Taking a moment to reflect on our own experiences can help us connect with our kids and communicate better.

- **Recognizing Patterns**: It's important to notice if we're repeating the same misunderstandings with our kids that we experienced with our parents, so we can stop the cycle.

- **Changing Emotional Needs**: As our kids grow from teenagers to adults, their emotional needs evolve, and we need to adapt how we support and talk to them.

- **Impact of Financial Situation**: Our financial stability, education, and career goals play a big part in our decisions about family size and timing.

- **Evolving Gender Roles**: Traditional roles are changing, with more shared parenting responsibilities and dads taking on more active roles.

- **Understanding Our Motivations**: Thinking about why we decided to have kids can give us insights into our parenting style and help improve our relationships with our children.

- **Building Empathy**: By understanding and addressing our kids' emotional needs, we can create a more supportive and understanding family environment.

Chapter 2: The Misconception of Parental Expectations

Unrealistic Expectations and Their Consequences

Parents often dream big for their children, envisioning them as future doctors, lawyers, or entrepreneurs who will achieve remarkable success, happiness, and stability. While these dreams can be motivating, they often place a heavy burden on their sons and daughters. These high expectations are frequently not just about the child's potential but are rooted in the parents' own unfulfilled ambitions. It's as if parents are attempting to relive their lives through their children, hoping they will succeed where the parents themselves could not.

Imagine a parent who always aspired to be a doctor but had to abandon that dream due to circumstances beyond their control. This parent might push their son or daughter toward a medical career, irrespective of their own interests and passions. The son or daughter, eager to please and live up to these expectations, might feel immense pressure, leading to stress and anxiety. Instead of exploring their own path, they end up carrying the weight of their parents' unmet goals, which can stifle their own dreams and potential.

The Burden of Sons and Daughters Caring for Parents in Old Age

In many cultures, it's almost an unspoken rule that children will take care of their parents as they grow older. This expectation can nurture a loving family dynamic, fostering close-knit bonds and mutual support. However, it can also become a heavy burden when it turns from a voluntary act of love into an obligatory duty.

Consider an adult son or daughter balancing a demanding career, their own family, and the added responsibility of caring for aging parents. The pressure to fulfill this duty can be overwhelming, leading to feelings of guilt and resentment. Parents, perhaps unknowingly, might expect their sons and daughters to prioritize their care, not fully appreciating the impact on their children's lives.

This expectation often springs from a place of fear—fear of being alone, losing independence, or becoming a burden. While it's natural to desire support in old age, it's crucial to recognize that expecting it as a given can strain relationships. Sons and daughters may feel trapped, torn between their love for their parents and their need for personal space and time. The resulting tension can create a rift, making the situation more difficult for everyone involved.

However, it's important to clarify that there is nothing more noble than a son or daughter reciprocating the love and care they received from their parents. Taking care of elderly parents can be a beautiful and fulfilling experience, fostering deep connections and gratitude. The issue arises when this care is expected as an obligation, leading to a cycle of guilt and pressure.

The Selfishness of Expecting Reciprocal Care

Expecting sons and daughters to care for their parents simply because "it's what families do" can seem selfish. It overlooks their right to lead their own lives, make their own choices, and pursue their own dreams. This expectation is often rooted in parents' anxieties about aging and dependency.

Picture a parent, fearing loneliness in old age, constantly reminding their son or daughter of the "duty" to care for them. This can create a profound sense of obligation and guilt, leading the son or daughter to feel as if they have no choice but to comply. The parent, perhaps unintentionally, projects their fears and needs onto their child, not realizing the emotional toll it takes.

This dynamic can lead to a cycle of guilt and pressure. The son or daughter, feeling obligated, may neglect their own needs and aspirations, while the parent remains unaware of the sacrifice being made. Over time, this can damage the relationship, breeding resentment and emotional distance. What starts as a fear of being a burden ends up creating a burden, leading to strained family ties and unfulfilled lives on both sides.

Different Parenting Styles and Their Impact

Understanding different parenting styles is crucial to comprehending how parental expectations and misunderstandings develop. Parenting styles are broadly categorized into four types: authoritative, authoritarian, permissive, and uninvolved. Each style has distinct characteristics and impacts on children.

Authoritative Parenting

Think of authoritative parenting as the gold standard—it's about finding that sweet spot between being supportive and having high expectations. Authoritative parents set clear rules, but they also encourage open communication and independence. This approach usually fosters a positive environment where children feel secure yet free to express themselves.

However, even authoritative parents can fall into the trap of overprotection. Picture a scenario where you, as a parent, fear your child's failure so deeply that you end up controlling more aspects of their life than necessary. Your intention is good—you want them to succeed—but this can sometimes stifle their independence and self-confidence. The key is to balance guidance with letting them make their own mistakes and learn from them.

Authoritarian Parenting

Authoritarian parents take a "my way or the highway" approach. They enforce strict rules and expect obedience without question. This style often stems from a desire for control and a fear of failure, which can result in children feeling oppressed and misunderstood.

If you find yourself frequently laying down the law without room for discussion, it might be worth considering how this impacts your child. While discipline is important, a lack of open communication can prevent your child from developing their own voice and expressing their individuality. They might comply out of fear rather than understanding, leading to potential rebellion or withdrawal in the long run.

Permissive Parenting

Permissive parents are the easy-going ones who avoid setting firm boundaries. This approach often comes from a desire to be liked by their children and to avoid conflict. While it might seem like you're being the cool parent, permissiveness can lead to misunderstandings when children lack the guidance and discipline they need.

Imagine your child staying up late on school nights because you don't want to argue about bedtime. They might enjoy the freedom initially, but over time, they may struggle with responsibility and boundaries. Children need structure to feel secure, and without it, they might find it difficult to navigate life's challenges.

Uninvolved Parenting

Uninvolved parents are detached, providing little guidance or support. This style often results from unresolved personal issues or a fear of judgment, leading to neglect of the child's emotional and developmental needs. Children of uninvolved parents may feel neglected and develop issues with self-worth and independence.

If you're dealing with your own struggles, it's easy to become disconnected from your child's life. Maybe you're swamped with work or dealing with personal stress. However, it's important to recognize how this detachment affects your child. They need your attention and support to develop a healthy sense of self and confidence. Taking small steps to engage more can make a big difference in their development and emotional well-being.

Heart-to-Heart with Fellow Parents: Practical Tips for Each Parenting Style

As parents, we all strive to do what's best for our children, but it's crucial to reflect on how our parenting style impacts them, even as they become adults. It's not about being perfect—no one is—but about being aware and adaptable. Let's have a heart-to-heart about how we can make small changes that can lead to big improvements in our relationships with our grown-up sons and daughters.

Authoritative Parents

If you consider yourself an authoritative parent, you're already doing a lot right by balancing high expectations with support and understanding. But even in this style, there's room for growth. Sometimes, in our eagerness to guide, we might hover a bit too closely.

Imagine your adult son or daughter is making a significant life decision, like choosing a career path or buying a house. Instead of immediately steering them towards what you think is best, take a step back and listen. Ask them about their thoughts and what excites or concerns them about their options. This not only helps them feel heard but also builds their confidence in making decisions.

Make it a habit to have these kinds of conversations. Regular check-ins can be a simple, effective way to ensure your son or daughter feels supported. Over a coffee or during a walk, ask them about their current challenges and triumphs. Show genuine interest in their thoughts and feelings. This open line of communication will foster a sense of security and trust.

Authoritarian Parents

For those of us who lean towards an authoritarian style, the challenge is to soften the edges a bit. It's about finding ways to maintain authority while also being approachable and supportive.

Think about the last time you gave advice or laid down a rule. Did you explain why it was important, or was it more of a "because I said so" moment? Next time, try explaining the reasoning behind your advice or expectations. This can turn a potentially contentious situation into a collaborative discussion.

Also, consider incorporating regular family meetings or discussions where everyone gets a chance to voice their opinions and concerns. It's a way to show your grown-up children that their voices matter and that your expectations come from a place of care and thoughtfulness, not just authority.

Permissive Parents

Permissive parents, your strength lies in your kindness and flexibility, but sometimes this can lead to a lack of structure. Adult children might enjoy the freedom but often need guidance and boundaries to feel supported.

Picture this: your adult daughter wants to make a significant investment or career change. Instead of avoiding the conflict or letting her make potentially risky decisions unchecked, offer your guidance. Help her weigh the pros and cons, and provide constructive feedback.

Creating a framework for these discussions can be incredibly beneficial. It doesn't have to be rigid, but a bit of structure—like setting clear financial goals or career plans—can provide a sense of stability. This helps them manage their responsibilities better and understand the importance of thoughtful planning.

Uninvolved Parents

For those who find themselves more uninvolved, perhaps due to personal struggles or demanding schedules, the key is to reconnect with your adult child's life in small but meaningful ways.

Start with simple actions. Spend time engaging in activities your son or daughter enjoys, whether it's discussing their favorite books, attending their social events, or just having a deep conversation. Show up for their important moments and be present in their lives.

Ask open-ended questions about their goals, their friends, and their passions. This shows that you care and are invested in their lives. It might feel awkward at first if you're not used to it, but consistency will help bridge the gap. Your interest and presence can make a significant difference in their emotional well-being.

Unconscious Influences on Parenting

Let's revisit the idea of unrealistic expectations and the projection of one's dreams, as mentioned earlier. As parents, we often have the best intentions for our children, but it's easy to overlook how our unconscious thoughts and feelings shape our interactions and expectations. There are several subtle yet powerful forces at play that can lead to misunderstandings and tensions. Let's delve into some of these influences and see how they affect our relationships with our grown-up children.

Projection of Dreams and Aspirations

Have you ever found yourself pushing your son or daughter toward a particular career or life path? This might be because, on some level, you're projecting your own unfulfilled dreams onto them. Perhaps you always wanted to be an artist, a doctor, or a successful entrepreneur, but life took you in a different direction. Without realizing it, you might be hoping your child will achieve what you couldn't.

Take, for instance, a parent who always dreamed of playing professional sports but had to give it up due to an injury. Now, this parent might sign their child up for every sports camp and training session, fervently cheering them on from the sidelines. The child, on the other hand, might be more interested in music or science. This can create immense pressure for them, especially if their passions lie elsewhere. The child may feel obligated to pursue a path they're not passionate about just to make their parent proud.

Instead, try to support their own aspirations, even if they differ from your own. If your child loves painting instead of playing soccer, encourage their creativity. Attend their art shows with the same enthusiasm you would a game. Celebrate their unique interests and help them pursue what truly makes them happy. Your support will mean the world to them and will help them grow into confident individuals.

Fear of Failure

We all fear seeing our children struggle or fail. It's natural. But sometimes, this fear can make us overprotective, leading us to control their choices more than we should. For example, if you're constantly advising your child against taking risks, you might be stifling their independence and self-discovery.

Imagine your daughter wants to start her own business. The idea excites her, but you, worried about the risks, keep pushing her to find a "safer" job with a stable income. While your intentions are good, you might be hindering her entrepreneurial spirit. She needs to experience the ups and downs to learn resilience and problem-solving.

Failures and mistakes are valuable learning experiences that help them grow. Trust in their ability to navigate their own path, even if it means watching them stumble along the way. Support them by offering guidance when they seek it and being a source of encouragement, not a roadblock.

Desire for Control

Let's face it—parenting can sometimes feel like a balancing act between guiding and controlling. An unconscious desire to maintain control and authority can result in setting strict rules and high expectations. This often causes friction as your children seek their own autonomy.

Consider a parent who meticulously plans out their child's education and career path. Every decision, from which college to attend to which major to choose, is heavily influenced by the parent's preferences. This can lead to tension and rebellion, as the child feels their own desires are being overshadowed.

It's important to recognize when your need for control might be overstepping and to start loosening the reins. Encourage open dialogue and let them make more of their own decisions, even if it's tough to watch from the sidelines. Trust that you've given them a good foundation and allow them the space to grow.

Need for Validation

It's not uncommon for parents to seek validation through their children's successes. Whether it's academic achievements, career milestones, or social accolades, there's a part of us that feels validated when our children do well.

Think about the pride you feel when your son graduates with honors or your daughter lands a prestigious job. While celebrating their successes is important, it's equally important to recognize their efforts and support them when they fall short. If they feel that your love and approval are contingent on their achievements, they may experience undue pressure and stress.

Celebrate their successes, of course, but also show them that your pride and love are unconditional. Recognize their efforts and growth, regardless of the outcome. Their worth—and yours—is not tied to these external markers of success.

Generational Conditioning

Many of our parenting styles and values are inherited from how we were raised. If your parents had a strict, no-nonsense approach, you might find yourself doing the same, even if it doesn't fit with today's parenting philosophies.

For instance, if you were raised with the belief that discipline and hard work are paramount, you might push your child to excel in these areas. But if your child thrives in a more nurturing and supportive environment, this approach might not be effective.

Reflect on whether these inherited values align with modern perspectives and your child's unique needs. Sometimes, breaking away from generational conditioning can lead to healthier, more adaptive parenting. Embrace flexibility and be willing to adapt your methods to better suit your child's personality and the evolving world around them.

Fear of Judgment

Let's talk about the fear of judgment. It's something we all feel at times, especially when it comes to parenting. We look around at other parents, compare ourselves, and sometimes even feel inadequate. This concern can lead us to impose certain behaviors and achievements on our children just to appear successful or to avoid criticism.

Imagine you're at a family gathering and everyone is bragging about their children's accomplishments. You might feel pressured to highlight your child's achievements, or worse, push them to excel in areas they might not be interested in just to keep up appearances. This can create a lot of stress for both you and your child. Instead, focus on celebrating their unique talents and interests. Your child's happiness and well-being are far more important than meeting societal expectations.

Unresolved Personal Issues

We all have our own baggage—unresolved insecurities or past traumas that can unintentionally spill over into our parenting. Maybe you were criticized harshly as a child and now, without realizing it, you're overly critical of your own children. Or perhaps you faced rejection and now fear that your child will experience the same pain.

This projection can create misunderstandings and strain your relationship. It's essential to recognize these patterns and work through them, perhaps with the help of a therapist. By addressing your own issues, you can avoid projecting them onto your children, fostering a healthier and more supportive dynamic.

Over-identification

It's natural to see a bit of ourselves in our children, but problems arise when we see them as extensions of ourselves rather than as independent individuals. This over-identification can lead to conflicts and misunderstandings.

For example, if you were a star athlete in high school, you might push your child to excel in sports, expecting them to match or surpass your achievements. But what if they're more interested in music or science? Recognize and celebrate their individuality. Your children are their own people with their own dreams and talents. Support them in their chosen paths, and you'll both be happier for it.

Subconscious Anxiety

We all worry about our children's futures, but sometimes this subconscious anxiety can lead to overprotectiveness or excessive control. Maybe you're constantly checking in on them, making decisions for them, or setting strict rules because you're anxious about what might happen if you don't.

While it's natural to want to protect your children, it's also important to let them learn from their own experiences. Trust in the values and skills you've taught them. Allowing them to face challenges and make mistakes is crucial for their development and independence.

Difficulty Letting Go

Watching your children grow up and become independent can be bittersweet. It's hard to let go, but holding on too tightly can create resistance to their autonomy. Maybe you're still trying to manage their schedules, make decisions for them, or solve their problems even when they're capable of doing it themselves.

Recognize this struggle within yourself. It's okay to feel this way, but try to step back and give them space to grow. Encourage them to take on more responsibilities and make their own choices. This will help them build confidence and independence.

Idealized Image of Childhood

We all have memories of our own childhoods, some of which we cherish and want to recreate for our children. However, imposing an idealized image of childhood based on our experiences can lead to unrealistic expectations and misunderstandings.

For instance, if you loved playing a certain sport or instrument as a child, you might push your child to do the same, even if they're not interested. It's important to realize that your child's experiences and interests will be different from yours. Embrace their unique journey and support them in discovering what makes them happy.

Misinterpretation of Behavior

Unconscious biases can sometimes cause us to misinterpret our children's behavior as defiance or disrespect, rather than expressions of individuality or stress. For example, if your child is quiet and withdrawn, you might see it as disobedience, when in fact, they might be feeling overwhelmed or anxious.

Try to understand the underlying reasons for their behavior. Open up a dialogue and listen to their concerns. This approach can help you build a more empathetic and supportive relationship.

Unconscious Competition

It's not uncommon to feel a bit of competition with your growing children, especially as they start achieving things that maybe you didn't. This unconscious competition can lead to conflicts and strain your relationship.

For instance, if your child excels academically or professionally in ways you didn't, you might feel a mix of pride and jealousy. Acknowledge these feelings and focus on celebrating their achievements without comparing them to your own. Their success is not a reflection on your past but a testament to their hard work and your support.

Boys vs. Girls

Let's talk about the different expectations we often place on boys and girls. Have you ever noticed how society and even our families push boys towards competitive sports and leadership roles? They're encouraged to be assertive and take charge. Meanwhile, girls might be steered towards excelling in academics and upholding certain social standards, like being polite and nurturing.

These gendered expectations can box our kids into traditional roles, limiting their potential. Imagine a boy who loves painting but feels he has to play football to fit in, or a girl who dreams of being an engineer but feels pressured to focus on softer subjects. It's crucial for us as parents to recognize these stereotypes and challenge them. Let's give our children the freedom to explore their passions, whatever they may be, regardless of gender.

Comparative Expectations

Now, let's explore the dynamics between siblings. When parents start comparing their kids, it can really shake things up in the family. Picture this: one child is constantly praised for their straight A's while the other, who excels in sports, feels overshadowed. This can lead to sibling rivalry, resentment, and even feelings of favoritism.

Both kids suffer in this scenario. The "star" child might feel immense pressure to maintain their high standards, fearing failure. Meanwhile, the other child may struggle with self-esteem, always feeling like they're in their sibling's shadow. It's so important for parents to appreciate and celebrate each child's unique strengths and achievements. Let's avoid comparisons and support our kids for who they truly are.

Attachment Issues

Deep-rooted attachment issues can make it hard to let go emotionally, causing you to cling to your children even as they seek independence. This can create tension and make it difficult for them to establish their own identities.

Work on building a relationship that respects their need for independence while maintaining a strong emotional connection. This balance can help them feel supported without feeling smothered.

Fear of Loss

We all have that underlying fear of losing our children's love and affection as they grow older and more independent. This fear can sometimes make us act in ways that are overbearing or intrusive. Maybe you find yourself constantly texting them to check in, or perhaps you're tempted to weigh in on their personal decisions more than they'd like.

But here's the thing: trust the bond you've built with your children over the years. Love and respect don't diminish with space; in fact, they grow stronger. It's like a plant—you give it space to grow, but you're always there to support it with what it needs. Show your children that you believe in their ability to make good choices and that you'll always be there for them, no matter what. This confidence in their independence will reinforce their trust and appreciation for you.

Fostering Healthier Relationships

Understanding these unconscious influences is crucial for building healthier, more supportive relationships with your grown-up children. By recognizing and addressing these underlying issues, you can better support their growth and independence, creating more harmonious family dynamics.

Take a moment to reflect on these insights. Are there areas where you might be projecting your own fears or dreams onto your children? Are there patterns of control or anxiety that you can start to change? Small adjustments in how you interact can make a big difference.

Embrace open conversations, encourage their independence, and celebrate their unique paths. Show them that they are valued for who they are, not just for their achievements. By being mindful and open to change, you'll find that your relationship with your children flourishes in new and unexpected ways.

Remember, parenting is a journey that evolves as our children grow. Let's continue to learn and adapt, ensuring that our children feel loved and supported, every step of the way.

Highlights of The Chapter

In this chapter, we dive into how our big dreams for our kids can sometimes become heavy burdens for them. We talk about how our own unfulfilled ambitions might influence our expectations, and how this can put a lot of pressure on our children. We also look at the tricky balance of expecting our kids to take care of us as we age and how this can create feelings of guilt and resentment. By reflecting on different parenting styles and our own unconscious motivations, we can start to build healthier, more supportive relationships with our children.

Key Points to Take Away

- **Big Dreams, Big Pressures**: We all want the best for our kids, but sometimes our dreams for them are really about our own unmet goals. It's important to recognize this and make sure we're not putting too much pressure on them.

- **Caring for Aging Parents**: It's natural to want our kids to look after us when we're older, but it can become a heavy burden if it feels more like an obligation than a choice. Balancing love and duty is key.

- **Parenting Styles**: Understanding whether you're more authoritative, authoritarian, permissive, or uninvolved can help you see how your parenting style affects your kids and find a healthy balance.

- **Following Their Own Path**: Encourage your kids to pursue their own interests, even if they're different from what you envisioned. Support them in finding their own passions and dreams.

- **Letting Them Fail**: It's hard to see our kids struggle, but letting them make mistakes and learn from them is crucial for their growth and independence.

- **Unconditional Love**: Show your kids that you love and are proud of them for who they are, not just for their achievements. This helps them feel secure and valued.

- **Adapting with the Times**: Parenting styles from our own childhood might not always fit today's world. Be open to change and adapt your approach to meet your child's needs.

- **Giving Them Space**: Trust your kids to make their own decisions and give them the space to grow. Being there for them when they need you is what matters most.

- **Breaking Gender Norms**: Encourage your children to explore their interests without being limited by traditional gender roles. Support them in whatever they choose to do.

- **Avoid Comparisons**: Celebrate each child's unique strengths and avoid comparing them to their siblings. This helps them build self-esteem and reduces sibling rivalry.

- **Building Independence**: Understand your own fears and attachment issues, and work on giving your kids the freedom they need while maintaining a strong bond.

Chapter 3: Mindful Parenting

Parenting is often compared to walking a tightrope. The balancing act between guiding your children and giving them the space to grow can be precarious. What if the secret to finding this balance lies not in maintaining constant vigilance, but in practicing mindful parenting? This chapter delves into the transformative power of mindfulness in your parenting journey.

What is Mindful Parenting?

Imagine for a moment you are in a bustling park. Laughter fills the air, and people are scattered across the green expanse, some watching attentively, others buried in their phones. Now, picture yourself as one of these people. You're fully present, your senses tuned to the environment. You notice the subtle shifts in your son or daughter's demeanor, the joy in their eyes as they talk about their day, the slight hesitation before they share a concern. This is the essence of mindful parenting—being fully present and engaged in the moment with your son or daughter.

Mindful parenting isn't about perfection. It's about connection. It's recognizing that every interaction, every conversation, is an opportunity to understand your child better and to foster a deeper bond.

Theoretical Foundations

Interested in the science behind mindful parenting? It's fascinating how this approach doesn't just alter daily interactions but also has a profound impact on the brain. Here's a deeper look into the psychological and neuroscientific foundations that support mindful parenting.

One of the most groundbreaking scientific concepts in recent decades is **neural plasticity**—the brain's ability to change and adapt throughout life. Mindfulness practices enhance this plasticity by strengthening neural pathways that promote focus, calm, and rational thinking. Regular mindfulness exercises can effectively rewire the brain to be more resilient to stress and more capable of managing emotional upheaval.

Engaging in mindfulness affects the hypothalamic-pituitary-adrenal (HPA) axis, which is crucial in **regulating our stress response**. Studies have shown that mindfulness can lower cortisol levels, the hormone associated with stress. For parents, this means better stress management, less reactivity to triggers in the parenting journey, and more reasoned responses to children's behaviors and emotions.

Mindfulness directly stimulates the prefrontal cortex, an area of the brain involved in **executive function**, which includes skills like impulse control, decision-making, and problem-solving. When parents practice mindfulness, they improve their own executive functions, leading not only to better parenting decisions but also modeling these critical skills for their children.

Mindful parenting helps to **quiet the amygdala**, the part of the brain that initiates our fight-or-flight response. This quieting effect makes room for the more thoughtful parts of the brain, like the prefrontal cortex, to take over and manage our reactions. This means less yelling or emotional outbursts and more maintaining composure in challenging parenting moments.

Mindfulness increases the production of serotonin and dopamine, **neurotransmitters** that boost mood and provide a sense of happiness and well-being. This biochemical change not only helps parents feel better emotionally but also impacts their interactions with their children, promoting a more positive home environment.

The benefits extend to children as well. When children grow up in an environment where mindfulness is practiced, their **neural development is influenced positively**, promoting better emotional regulation and social skills. This equips them with better tools to handle their own stress and build healthier relationships.

In essence, mindful parenting is not just a technique; it's a scientifically supported approach that enhances brain function in both parents and children, fostering a healthier, more harmonious family dynamic. Understanding these principles helps parents appreciate the profound impact of their efforts. Now, let's focus on the practical aspects. While the next chapter will cover communication techniques, this section will concentrate on practical strategies for being a mindful parent.

Observation and Listening

The first step in mindful parenting is to observe and listen. Sounds simple, right? Yet, in the hustle and bustle of daily life, how often do we truly see and hear our children?

Consider a typical evening at home. You ask your son or daughter about their day, expecting the usual "fine" or "okay." But what if you approached the conversation differently? What if you paused, looked into their eyes, and asked, "What was something that made you smile today?" This small change shifts the focus from a routine question to an invitation for meaningful dialogue.

Listening goes beyond hearing words. It involves paying attention to non-verbal cues—the slump of their shoulders, the sparkle in their eyes, the tone of their voice. These subtle signals often speak louder than words, revealing emotions and thoughts that might otherwise go unnoticed.

Moving Beyond Surface-Level Interactions

Mindful parenting encourages us to dig deeper, to move beyond surface-level interactions. It's about transforming those everyday exchanges into opportunities for genuine connection. Instead of sticking to the usual, "How was work today?" try something like, "Tell me about something interesting that happened at work today." This small tweak invites them to open up and share more, leading to richer, more meaningful conversations.

Show genuine curiosity by taking an interest in their hobbies, friendships, and opinions. Ask about their favorite music, what they're reading, or what they're excited about in their lives. This applies to both younger and adult children. Maybe your teenager is into a new band, or your adult daughter is reading a fascinating book. Ask them about it.

When they respond, really listen. Nod, maintain eye contact, and use verbal affirmations like "I see" or "That's interesting." This shows that you're engaged and truly care about what they're saying. For instance, if your son mentions he's started a new project at work, follow up with questions about it. Or if your daughter talks about a recent outing with friends, express interest in hearing the details.

These deeper interactions do more than just fill the silence; they make your sons and daughters feel heard and appreciated. They know that you're not just asking out of obligation, but because you genuinely care about their lives and what makes them tick. It's this kind of mindful engagement that strengthens your bond and fosters a sense of trust and understanding.

Creating Emotional Safety

Creating emotional safety is about making your kids, whether young or adult, feel loved and accepted for who they are. It means ensuring they feel secure enough to express themselves without fear of judgment.

Make your home a judgment-free zone. Encourage your kids to share their thoughts and feelings openly, and respond with empathy. Let them know it's okay to feel a range of emotions—joy, sadness, anger, or fear. Simple phrases like, "I understand why that would make you upset," or "It sounds like you're really excited about that!" can make them feel heard and understood.

Show them how to handle emotions by sharing your own feelings. If you had a tough day, say, "I felt really stressed today, but talking about it helps." This teaches them that expressing emotions is healthy and normal.

Trust is crucial. Be consistent in your actions and words. If you promise to spend time together, follow through. This reliability helps them feel secure and confident that they can count on you.

Support your kids in making their own decisions and solving their own problems. When they come to you with a problem, ask what they think might work instead of jumping in with a solution. This boosts their confidence and helps them feel capable and strong.

Celebrate their achievements and encourage them when they face challenges. Show them your love and support are unconditional. When they stumble, offer a hand, not a scolding.

Introduce simple mindfulness practices to help your kids stay present and manage their emotions. Activities like deep breathing, short meditations, or quiet moments together can make a big difference.

Practical Steps to Mindful Parenting

1. **Breathe and Be Present**: Before engaging with your son or daughter, take a few deep breaths to center yourself. This simple practice helps you become fully present.

2. **Active Listening**: Listen without interrupting. Show that you're paying attention through nodding, maintaining eye contact, and using encouraging words like "I see" or "Tell me more."

3. **Reflective Responses**: Reflect back what your son or daughter has said to show you understand. For instance, "It sounds like you had a tough day at work."

4. **Empathy Over Solutions**: Sometimes, people don't need solutions; they need empathy. Instead of immediately trying to fix a problem, acknowledge their feelings: "I can see why that would upset you."

5. **Open-Ended Questions**: Encourage deeper conversation with questions that can't be answered with a simple yes or no. "What was the best part of your day?" or "How did that make you feel?"

6. **Mindful Breaks**: Incorporate short mindfulness ex-

ercises into your daily routine. These could be moments of silence, guided meditation, or deep breathing exercises done together.

Building a Mindful Relationship

Mindful parenting is a journey, not a destination. It requires patience, practice, and a willingness to grow alongside your son or daughter. The rewards are profound: a stronger, more empathetic relationship, and a deeper understanding of the unique individual your child is becoming.

Recognizing and Valuing True Feelings

Recognizing and valuing your child's true feelings is essential for building a strong, empathetic relationship. This means acknowledging their emotions, even if you don't fully understand or agree with them. Validation doesn't necessarily mean you have to agree with their perspective; it's about respecting their feelings and letting them know that it's okay to feel the way they do.

For example, if your son or daughter is upset about a situation at work, instead of saying, "It's not a big deal," try saying, "I can see that this is really bothering you." This simple act of validation can make a significant difference in how they feel understood and supported.

Normalizing Emotions and Showing Empathy

Validation also means normalizing their emotions. Let them know that it's okay to feel angry, sad, or frustrated. Emotions are a natural part of being human, and by acknowledging this, you help your child accept and manage their feelings. If your son or daughter is angry because of a setback, instead of downplaying it by saying, "You'll get over it," try, "It's completely understandable to feel disappointed. It's something you really cared about."

Empathy is key. Put yourself in their shoes and try to see the world from their perspective. If your child is anxious about an upcoming project, think back to a time when you felt similar pressure. Share that memory with them to show that you can relate to their experience. You might say, "I remember feeling really nervous before my big presentations at work. It's natural to feel that way when something is important to you."

Individual Needs and Patience

Each son or daughter is unique. What works for one may not work for another. One might need a lot of verbal reassurance, while another might find comfort in a hug or quiet companionship. Pay attention to their individual cues and respond accordingly. If your son or daughter withdraws when upset, give them space but let them know you're there when they're ready to talk.

Be patient. Building a trusting, empathetic relationship takes time. There will be moments when you might not get it right, and that's okay. The important thing is to keep trying and to show your son or daughter that their feelings matter to you.

By practicing mindful parenting, asking meaningful questions, and valuing your child's true feelings, you create a nurturing environment where they feel safe, understood, and loved. This approach not only strengthens your relationship but also helps your children grow into confident, emotionally intelligent individuals.

So, take a deep breath, embrace the present moment, and embark on this path of mindful parenting. Your son or daughter is waiting for you to truly see and hear them.

Highlights of The Chapter

Chapter 3 explores the impact of mindful parenting on strengthening parent-child relationships. It defines this approach as being fully attentive and present, keenly observing a child's subtle emotions and behaviors, and responding with empathy. Key practices include active listening, recognizing non-verbal cues, and engaging beyond superficial interactions to develop deeper connections. The chapter also emphasizes establishing an emotional safety net, where children feel valued and safe to express themselves without judgment. Through these methods, parents can create a nurturing environment that fosters mutual respect and a deep, empathetic bond.

Key Points to Take Away

- **Presence in Interactions:** Be fully present during interactions, focusing intently on your child's words and behaviors to strengthen your connection.

- **Scientific Benefits:** Mindful parenting positively impacts the brain, enhancing neural plasticity, reducing stress, and improving emotional regulation and decision-making abilities.

- **Active Listening:** Engage in active listening, which involves observing non-verbal cues and responding with empathy, showing genuine interest in what your child is communicating.

- **Deeper Conversations:** Move beyond routine questions to ask more thoughtful ones that invite meaningful responses and show that you value their thoughts and experiences.

- **Emotional Safety:** Create a safe emotional space by responding to your child's feelings with understanding and without judgment, reinforcing their comfort in expressing emotions.

- **Empathy Over Solutions:** Focus on empathy rather than immediate solutions when addressing your child's concerns, which helps them feel supported and understood.

- **Reflective Responses:** Use reflective responses to demonstrate that you are listening and understanding your child's perspective, deepiing the communicative bond.

- **Encourage Expression:** Encourage your child to articulate their feelings and decisions, supporting them in becoming more self-aware and confident in their ability to solve problems.

- **Mindful Practices:** Incorporate simple mindfulness exercises into daily routines to help both you and your child remain centered and connected.

Chapter 4: Effective Communication

Continuing from the mindful parenting principles explored in Chapter 3, this chapter transitions to focus on the subtleties of effective communication with children of all ages. Effective communication transcends simple exchanges; it is foundational to deepening understanding and strengthening the bonds between parents and children, whether they are young or fully grown. Building on the importance of being present and attentive, we will now delve into how to articulate our understanding and foster an open, respectful dialogue. This chapter will guide you through essential communication skills, active listening techniques, and non-judgmental responses, aiming to enhance the empathetic communication pathways with your children throughout their lives.

Foundations of Communication: Building Blocks for Effective Dialogue

Communication is the lifeblood of any relationship, and this is especially true for the bond between parents and their children, whether they are young or adults. The foundation of effective communication lies in mutual respect and understanding. It's about creating a dialogue where both parties feel valued and heard.

Effective communication begins with the basics—tone, body language, and choice of words. Imagine speaking with a friend; you naturally use a gentle tone, maintain eye contact, and choose your words carefully to ensure your message is clear and respectful. The same principles apply when communicating with your children, regardless of their age.

A key building block of effective communication is empathy. Empathy allows you to understand and share the feelings of your children. It helps in bridging the gap between your experiences and theirs, making your conversations more meaningful and connected. Start by acknowledging their emotions, even if you don't fully understand them. Phrases like "I see you're upset" or "It sounds like that was really difficult for you" can go a long way in making your children feel heard and understood.

Another essential element is patience. Whether your children are struggling to articulate their thoughts and feelings due to their youth or the complexities of adult life, giving them the time and space to express themselves without interruption or rush is crucial. This not only helps them communicate better but also builds their confidence in sharing with you.

Active Listening: Techniques to Truly Hear Your Kids

Active listening is more than just hearing words; it's about fully engaging with the speaker and understanding their message. When you practice active listening, you show your children that their thoughts and feelings are important to you.

Here are some techniques to enhance your active listening skills:

Focus Fully: Give your kids your undivided attention. Put away distractions like phones or TV and maintain eye contact. This signals that you are fully present and interested in what they have to say.

- **Practical Example**: When your adult child calls you to talk about a rough day at work, find a quiet space to sit down and listen. Turn off the TV, put your phone on silent, and focus on their voice and words.

Reflect and Clarify: Reflect back what you've heard to confirm understanding. For example, "So, you're feeling nervous about the project at work?" This not only shows that you're listening but also helps clarify any misunderstandings.

- **Practical Example**: If your teenage child is upset about a friend's behavior, you might say, "It sounds like you're hurt because your friend canceled your plans at the last minute. Is that right?"

Encourage Elaboration: Use prompts to encourage your children to elaborate on their thoughts. Questions like "What happened next?" or "How did that make you feel?" invite them to share more details and deepen the conversation.

- **Practical Example**: When your young adult child mentions feeling stressed about their college exams, ask, "Can you tell me more about what's making you feel this way?" or "What are some specific things that are worrying you?"

Validate Their Feelings: Acknowledge your children's emotions, even if you don't agree with their perspective. Phrases like "I can see why you'd feel that way" validate their experience and show empathy.

- **Practical Example**: If your adult child expresses frustration about a conflict with a co-worker, respond with, "I understand why you're upset. It's tough dealing with difficult people at work."

Summarize and Affirm: At the end of the conversation, summarize what you've heard and affirm your support. For instance, "It sounds like you had a tough day. I'm here for you, and we'll figure it out together."

- **Practical Example**: After listening to your teenager talk about their struggles with school, you might say, "You've been under a lot of pressure with your assignments and exams. I'm proud of how hard you're working, and I'm here to help you through this."

Non-Judgmental Responses: How to Respond Without Imposing Judgments

Imagine your son or daughter coming to you with something weighing heavily on their mind. They're opening up, hoping for understanding, but instead, they feel judged. It's a scenario that can shut down communication faster than anything else. When judgment creeps into the conversation, it creates an invisible wall, making them hesitant to share their true feelings in the future. This is why mastering the art of non-judgmental responses is so crucial.

Picture this: your son or daughter has finally built up the courage to talk about something deeply personal. They need a safe space, a haven where they can be vulnerable without fear of criticism or dismissal. Non-judgmental responses are about creating this safe space. It's not always easy, especially when emotions run high or the topic hits close to home. But with a few thoughtful approaches, you can transform these moments into opportunities for deeper connection and trust.

Non-judgmental responses allow your son or daughter to feel comfortable being honest and open with you. It's about listening with empathy, responding with care, and ensuring your reactions foster trust rather than erode it. By practicing these techniques, you can encourage more meaningful conversations and help your child feel truly heard and valued.

Here's how to practice non-judgmental responses:

Avoid Immediate Reactions: When your child shares something shocking or disappointing, resist the urge to react immediately. Take a moment to process and respond calmly.

- **Practical Example**: If your adult child tells you they are considering a major career change, take a deep breath and say, "That's a big decision. I'd love to hear more about why you're thinking of making this change."

Focus on Feelings, Not Behavior: Separate the child from their actions. Instead of saying "You're being irresponsible," try "I'm concerned about this situation because I know you're capable of doing better. What's going on?"

- **Practical Example**: If your teenager missed curfew, instead of scolding them immediately, say, "I was worried when you didn't come home on time. Can you tell me what happened?"

Ask Open-Ended Questions: Encourage exploration of their feelings and thoughts with open-ended questions. "Can you tell me more about what happened?" invites a detailed response, unlike "Why did you do that?" which can feel accusatory.

- **Practical Example**: If your adult child seems distant after a family gathering, ask, "Can you share how you felt during dinner last night?"

Express Understanding Before Offering Solutions: Show that you understand their perspective before jumping in with advice or solutions. "I understand that you're feeling frustrated with your job. Let's see if we can figure out a way to make it easier."

- **Practical Example**: When your college-aged child expresses anxiety about future career prospects, acknowledge their feelings with, "It's completely normal to feel uncertain about the future. What are some of your concerns?"

Be Mindful of Your Tone and Body Language: Ensure that your tone and body language align with a non-judgmental attitude. A gentle tone, relaxed posture, and open gestures communicate acceptance and understanding.

- **Practical Example**: During a heated conversation with your teenager, keep your voice calm and your body language open. Instead of crossing your arms or raising your voice, lean in slightly and speak softly to show you're there to listen, not judge.

Building Trust: Steps to Create a Trusting Relationship

Trust is the cornerstone of any strong relationship. Building trust with your children ensures that they feel safe coming to you with their problems, fears, and joys, no matter their age. Here's how you can foster a trusting relationship:

Consistency: Be consistent in your words and actions. Children need to know they can rely on you. If you promise to do something, follow through. Consistency builds a sense of security and reliability.

- **Practical Example**: If you tell your adult child you'll help them move on Saturday, make sure you show up. If you promise your teenager a trip to the mall, don't cancel last minute unless it's unavoidable. Consistency in small things makes a big difference.

- **Another Example**: If you always say "Good night" to your younger child at bedtime, continue this tradition with your older or adult children when they visit. It shows that some things never change, reinforcing a sense of reliability.

Transparency: Be honest with your children. If you make a mistake, acknowledge it. Apologizing and admitting when you're wrong models honesty and integrity.

- **Practical Example**: If you lose your temper and yell, go back to your child and say, "I'm sorry I raised my voice earlier. That wasn't fair to you." This shows them it's okay to admit faults and seek forgiveness.

- **Another Example**: If you can't attend an important event your child invites you to, explain why honestly instead of making excuses. "I really wanted to be there for your presentation, but I have a crucial meeting at work that I can't miss."

Respect Privacy: Respect your children's need for privacy and autonomy. This shows that you trust them and in turn, they are more likely to trust you.

- **Practical Example**: Knock before entering their room, whether they are a teenager or an adult living at home. If your adult child shares something personal with you, keep it confidential unless they give you permission to share it.

- **Another Example**: When your child confides in you about their personal life or relationships, avoid prying for more information than they're comfortable sharing. Respect their boundaries and let them share at their own pace.

Support Without Conditions: Show unconditional support. Let your children know that your love and support are not based on their achievements or behavior. This creates a foundation of trust that is not easily shaken.

- **Practical Example**: If your child fails a test or makes a mistake at work, reassure them with, "I love you and I'm here for you, no matter what. We'll figure this out together." This reinforces that your support isn't conditional on their success.

- **Another Example**: If your child decides to pursue a

career or life path that you wouldn't have chosen for them, support them anyway. "I might not understand everything about this career choice, but I believe in you and I'm here to help you succeed."

Encourage Independence: Trust them to make their own decisions and support them in the process. This not only builds their confidence but also shows that you trust their judgment.

- **Practical Example**: When your adult child is deciding on a career change, offer your advice if asked, but ultimately support their decision. "I trust that you know what's best for you, and I'm here to support you in whatever you choose."

- **Another Example**: Allow your teenager to plan a family outing or take charge of a household project. This demonstrates your trust in their abilities and decision-making skills.

Create Rituals: Establish regular routines or rituals that reinforce your bond. This could be a weekly game night, daily check-ins, or regular one-on-one time. These rituals create a sense of predictability and trust.

- **Practical Example**: Have a Sunday brunch tradition where you and your adult child catch up on each other's lives, or a nightly routine where you spend a few minutes talking with your teenager about their day before bed.

- **Another Example**: Start a book club with your children, where you all read the same book and discuss it weekly. This can be particularly engaging for adult children and promotes both connection and intellectual growth.

By integrating these foundations of communication, active listening techniques, non-judgmental responses, and trust-building steps into your parenting, you foster an environment where your children feel valued, understood, and safe. This chapter isn't just about improving dialogue; it's about transforming your relationship with your children into one rooted in mutual respect and deep connection, regardless of their age.

Communication Mistakes to Avoid with Your Sons and Daughters

When it comes to talking with your sons and daughters, it's not always easy to get it right. We've all had those moments where we think we're being clear or supportive, only to realize we've accidentally hurt feelings or shut down the conversation. Knowing the common communication mistakes can be a game-changer.

It's like having a map that helps you avoid the bumps and potholes on the road to meaningful conversations.

Why is this so important? Because communication is the foundation of any relationship, and the way we talk to our kids—whether they're still at home or out on their own—can either strengthen that bond or put up walls. Avoiding these mistakes isn't about being perfect; it's about being mindful and intentional. It's about creating an environment where your sons and daughters feel respected, understood, and valued. By steering clear of these common pitfalls, you're setting the stage for open, honest, and loving dialogue that can last a lifetime.

1. **Interrupting or Talking Over Them**

   - **Why It's a Mistake**: Interrupting your sons or daughters can make them feel unheard and unimportant. It signals that what you have to say is more important than their thoughts and feelings.

   - **What to Do Instead**: Practice active listening. Allow them to finish their sentences before responding. This shows respect for their opinions and encourages them to share more openly.

2. **Invalidating Their Feelings**

   - **Why It's a Mistake**: Saying things like "You

shouldn't feel that way" or "It's not a big deal" dismisses their emotions and can lead to a lack of trust and openness.

- **What to Do Instead**: Validate their feelings by acknowledging their emotions. Use phrases like "I understand that you're feeling upset" or "It's okay to feel that way."

3. Using Negative or Judgmental Language

- **Why It's a Mistake**: Harsh or critical language can damage your son's or daughter's self-esteem and hinder open communication. Words like "lazy," "stupid," or "irresponsible" can be particularly harmful.

- **What to Do Instead**: Focus on constructive feedback. Highlight the behavior you'd like to see changed without labeling or attacking their character. For example, say "I noticed you've been struggling with your homework. How can I help?" instead of "You're so lazy."

4. Comparing Them to Others

- **Why It's a Mistake**: Comparisons can breed resentment and feelings of inadequacy. It can make your sons or daughters feel like they're constantly being measured against others, which can harm their self-worth.

- **What to Do Instead**: Appreciate your son's or daughter's unique qualities and achievements. Encourage them to set and reach their own goals without comparing them to siblings, peers, or yourself.

5. **Imposing Your Solutions**

- **Why It's a Mistake**: Jumping in with solutions instead of allowing your son or daughter to solve their problems can make them feel incapable and dependent. It also shuts down open dialogue.

- **What to Do Instead**: Offer guidance and support while encouraging them to come up with their own solutions. Ask questions like "What do you think would be a good way to handle this?" or "How do you plan to approach this problem?"

6. **Not Practicing What You Preach**

- **Why It's a Mistake**: Sons and daughters are keen observers and often imitate the behavior of their parents. If there is a disconnect between your words and actions, it can lead to confusion and mistrust.

- **What to Do Instead**: Model the communication behaviors you want to see in your sons and daughters. Be consistent in your words and actions, and demonstrate the values you wish to instill.

7. **Neglecting Non-Verbal Cues**

- **Why It's a Mistake**: Body language, facial expressions, and tone of voice play a significant role in communication. Negative non-verbal cues can contradict your words and create misunderstandings.

- **What to Do Instead**: Be mindful of your non-verbal communication. Ensure your body language, eye contact, and tone of voice align with your verbal message to convey empathy and understanding.

8. **Failing to Apologize**

- **Why It's a Mistake**: Not apologizing when you're wrong can set a poor example and create a barrier in your relationship. It may lead your sons and daughters to feel that their feelings are not acknowledged or respected.

- **What to Do Instead**: Admit your mistakes and apologize sincerely. This shows humility and respect, and it teaches them the importance of taking responsibility for their actions.

9. **Being Inconsistent**

    - **Why It's a Mistake**: Inconsistency in rules, expectations, and responses can create confusion and insecurity. Sons and daughters need predictability to feel safe and understood.

    - **What to Do Instead**: Be consistent in your communication and actions. Clearly define and stick to your expectations and follow through on promises and consequences.

10. **Overloading with Information**

    - **Why It's a Mistake**: Giving too much information at once can overwhelm your sons and daughters and make it difficult for them to process and respond effectively.

    - **What to Do Instead**: Break down information into manageable chunks. Give them time to absorb and respond to each part before moving on.

Being aware of these common communication mistakes and actively avoiding them can really transform how you talk with your sons and daughters. By making these small but meaningful changes, you'll foster more positive and effective conversations. This effort goes a long way in not only strengthening your relationship but also in helping them grow into confident, communicative individuals.

The Impact of Technology on Communication

Before concluding this chapter on communication, it is almost mandatory to talk about technology. In today's world, technology plays a significant role in how children of all ages communicate and interact. As parents, it's important to understand and navigate this landscape to ensure we can connect with our children effectively.

Children today often turn to technology to communicate with their peers and express themselves. Social media, messaging apps, and online games provide platforms for interaction that were unimaginable a generation ago. While these tools offer opportunities for connection, they can also create challenges. Children might feel more comfortable sharing their thoughts and feelings online than face-to-face, sometimes leading to a sense of disconnection within the family.

For children who feel misunderstood or neglected, technology can become a refuge. They might retreat into the virtual world, seeking validation and companionship that they struggle to find offline. This makes it crucial for us as parents to bridge the gap between the digital and real worlds.

One way to do this is by showing interest in your child's online activities. Ask them about their favorite apps, games, or YouTube channels. Participate with them when possible, turning their digital interests into opportunities for bonding. This not only helps you understand their world better but also shows them that their interests matter to you.

For younger children, this might mean playing educational games together or watching age-appropriate videos. For teenagers, it could involve discussing their favorite social media platforms or joining them in online gaming sessions. Even with adult children, staying engaged with their digital lives by discussing the latest technology trends or apps they use can strengthen your connection.

It's also essential to set healthy boundaries around technology use. Encourage offline activities that promote direct interaction and emotional connection. Family dinners, game nights, and outdoor activities can help balance screen time with face-to-face communication.

Additionally, teach your children about the potential pitfalls of technology. Discuss the importance of privacy, the impact of social media on self-esteem, and the reality of cyberbullying. Empower them with the knowledge and skills to navigate the digital world safely and responsibly.

By understanding and integrating technology into our parenting, we can help our children feel more connected and supported. Remember, the goal is not to eliminate their digital lives but to enrich their overall well-being through balanced, meaningful interactions both online and offline.

Whether your child is a toddler just starting to explore educational apps, a teenager navigating social media, or an adult dealing with the demands of a digital workplace, staying engaged with their technological world is key. It's about creating an environment where they feel understood and supported, both in the virtual and real worlds.

Highlights of The Chapter

In this chapter, we have discussed the subtleties of effective communication with children of all ages. Building on mindful parenting principles, we emphasize the importance of understanding and respectful dialogue. We cover essential communication skills, active listening techniques, and non-judgmental responses. Additionally, we address common communication mistakes and the impact of technology on family interactions, offering practical strategies to enhance connections with your children.

Key Points to Take Away

- **Foundations of Communication**: Mutual respect and understanding are crucial. Use a gentle tone, eye contact, and careful word choice to ensure clear, respectful dialogue with your children.

- **Active Listening**: Techniques like focusing fully, reflecting, encouraging elaboration, validating feelings, and summarizing help you truly hear your kids and make them feel valued.

- **Non-Judgmental Responses**: Avoid immediate reactions, focus on feelings rather than behavior, ask open-ended questions, express understanding before offering solutions, and be mindful of your tone and body language to create a safe space for honest conversations.

- **Building Trust**: Consistency, transparency, respecting privacy, showing unconditional support, encouraging independence, and creating regular rituals foster a trusting relationship with your children.

- **Avoiding Communication Mistakes**: Don't interrupt, invalidate feelings, use negative language, compare, impose solutions, neglect non-verbal cues, fail to apologize, be inconsistent, or overload with information to ensure effective communication.

- **Impact of Technology**: Understand the role of technology in your children's lives. Show interest in their online activities, set healthy boundaries, and teach them about privacy, self-esteem, and cyberbullying to bridge the gap between digital and real-world interactions.

- **Practical Examples**: Apply communication techniques to real-life scenarios, whether dealing with young children, teenagers, or adult children, to foster effective dialogue and strengthen your relationship.

Chapter 5: Recognizing and Improving Parental Mistakes

Parenting teenagers and adult children presents unique challenges. By now, you're well aware that mistakes are part of the journey. What's important is how we handle those missteps—recognizing them, learning from them, and using them to improve our relationships with our children. This chapter is all about turning those inevitable parenting blunders into opportunities for growth. We'll discuss why admitting our mistakes is crucial and how doing so can strengthen the bond with our children. We'll also explore how our personal growth as parents benefits our sons and daughters. So, let's embrace our imperfections, learn from them, and move forward with greater understanding and love.

Identifying Common Parenting Mistakes

Let's be honest—no parent is perfect, and that's okay. Acknowledging that mistakes are part of the parenting journey is the first step towards growth. As parents of teenagers and adult children, it's essential to recognize these common missteps and understand their impact on our relationships. While some of these errors have been touched upon earlier in the book, it's fair to take them up individually and treat them properly.

Over-Scheduling Your Kids

In our fast-paced world, it's easy to fall into the trap of over-scheduling. As parents, we often feel the pressure to ensure our children have every opportunity to succeed and thrive. We want them to excel academically, athletically, and socially, so we fill their calendars with activities, lessons, and commitments. From soccer practice to piano lessons, debate club to dance class, our intentions are good—we want to provide a rich, diverse set of experiences that will help them grow and develop.

However, the reality of this well-meaning strategy can be quite different. Over-scheduling can lead to significant stress and burnout for both you and your children. When every hour of the day is accounted for, there's little room for spontaneity, rest, or simply being. Imagine your child, whether they are in school, college, or working, coming home exhausted from a full day, only to rush through their responsibilities and head off to a series of additional activities. This relentless pace can lead to physical and emotional exhaustion.

Beyond the immediate fatigue, over-scheduling can also impact your child's mental health. Constantly moving from one activity to another leaves little time for relaxation and self-reflection. It creates an ongoing sense of urgency and pressure to perform, which may contribute to anxiety and stress. Children might start to feel like they're constantly running a race they can never win, leading to feelings of inadequacy and frustration.

It's crucial to find a balance. Encourage downtime and free play, which are just as important for development and well-being as structured activities. Free play allows children to use their creativity, develop problem-solving skills, and build resilience. It also gives them the chance to unwind and process the events of their day.

Not Setting Boundaries

Being supportive and nurturing is vital, but so is respecting your children's boundaries. Without respecting these boundaries, parents can inadvertently cause their children—whether teenagers or adults—to struggle with trust, self-esteem, and independence. Boundaries provide the necessary structure and security, helping children develop self-discipline, responsibility, and a sense of respect.

Boundaries are like the guardrails on a winding mountain road; they keep us safe and on track. For children, clear boundaries help them understand what is expected of them and what behaviors are acceptable. This knowledge fosters a sense of security and predictability, which is crucial for emotional and psychological development. Without respecting boundaries, children may feel lost, anxious, and unsure of how to navigate their relationships and responsibilities.

Examples of Parental Boundary Violations:

- **Invading Privacy:** Parents enter their teenager's room without knocking or read their diaries and text messages.

    - **Impact:** This can lead to feelings of mistrust and resentment. Teenagers may feel their personal space and thoughts are not respected, leading to secrecy and a breakdown in communication.

- **Over-Involvement in Academic Choices:** Parents insist on choosing their daughter's college major or career path without considering her interests or strengths.

    - **Impact:** This can cause significant stress and dissatisfaction for the child, who may feel pressured to meet parental expectations rather than pursuing their own passions.

- **Controlling Social Life:** Parents dictate who their child can be friends with or whom they can date, often without reasonable cause.

    - **Impact:** This can result in social isolation and rebellion. The child may feel stifled and unable to develop healthy relationships independently.

- **Financial Control:** Even as adults, children find that their parents control their finances, dictating how they should spend their money or imposing conditions on financial support.

    - **Impact:** This can hinder the child's ability to develop financial independence and foster resentment and a sense of inadequacy.

- **Over-Scheduling Activities:** Parents fill every hour of their child's day with structured activities and lessons, leaving no time for rest or free play.

    - **Impact:** This can lead to burnout, stress, and a lack of creativity. The child may feel overwhelmed and lose interest in activities they once enjoyed.

- **Constant Criticism:** Parents consistently criticize their child's choices, appearance, or lifestyle, believing it will motivate improvement.

  - **Impact:** This can severely damage self-esteem and confidence. The child may feel they can never meet their parents' expectations, leading to anxiety and depression.

- **Ignoring Emotional Needs:** Parents focus solely on their child's academic or extracurricular achievements and neglect their emotional well-being.

  - **Impact:** The child may feel unloved and unsupported emotionally, leading to issues like depression, anxiety, and a strained parent-child relationship.

- **Lack of Respect for Adult Autonomy:** Parents continue to make decisions for their adult children, such as where they should live or work, without considering their desires.

  - **Impact:** This can lead to resentment and hinder the development of the child's own decision-making skills and independence.

Setting and enforcing appropriate boundaries consistently but kindly is crucial. Explain the reasons behind the rules, fostering respect and understanding rather than rebellion. Clear boundaries help children of all ages feel more secure, understood, and capable of navigating their world responsibly.

Comparing Siblings

Comparing your children, even with the best intentions, can be harmful. Each child, whether a teenager or an adult, is unique with their own strengths and challenges. Comparisons can lead to feelings of inadequacy, resentment, and sibling rivalry. Instead, celebrate each child's individual achievements and qualities, focusing on personal growth to nurture self-esteem and healthier sibling relationships.

Parents might not realize the subtle ways they compare their children, often in everyday statements that seem harmless but can have long-lasting negative effects. Here are some examples of mini negative sibling comparison statements and their potential impacts:

"Why can't you be more like your sister?"

Impact: This statement implies that one child is inferior to the other, fostering feelings of inadequacy and resentment. The child being compared might feel they can never meet the expectations set by their sibling's achievements.

"Your brother never had trouble with his homework."

Impact: This comparison can make a child feel less intelligent or capable, leading to a decline in self-esteem and motivation. It can also create tension between siblings, as one might feel unfairly burdened with being the standard.

"Look at how well your sister keeps her apartment clean. Why can't you do the same?"

Impact: This comment can make a child feel like they are constantly falling short, damaging their self-worth. It can also create animosity towards the sibling who is being praised, leading to rivalry and conflict.

"Your brother was always good at sports; you should try harder."

Impact: This type of comparison can discourage a child from pursuing their interests, feeling that their efforts will never be good enough. It can also create unnecessary pressure, causing stress and anxiety.

"I never have to remind your sister to do her chores."

Impact: This statement can make a child feel like they are a burden, fostering a negative self-image. It can also lead to a strained relationship with the sibling who is seen as more responsible.

"Your brother was already reading at your age."

Impact: Comparing developmental milestones can make a child feel inadequate and frustrated. Each child develops at their own pace, and such comparisons can undermine their confidence and interest in learning.

"Why can't you be as polite as your sister?"

Impact: This can make a child feel unloved and unappreciated for who they are. It can also cause resentment towards the sibling who is perceived as the "better" one.

Strategies to Avoid Negative Comparisons

- **Focus on Individual Strengths:** Highlight each child's unique talents and accomplishments. For example, instead of saying, "Why can't you get good grades like your brother?" say, "I really appreciate how hard you work on your projects. Your creativity is amazing."

- **Encourage Personal Growth:** Support each child's individual growth by setting personal goals that align with their interests and abilities. Celebrate their progress and efforts, regardless of how it compares to their siblings.

- **Use Positive Reinforcement:** Reinforce positive behavior and achievements with specific praise. For instance, "I'm really proud of how you handled that difficult situation. You showed a lot of maturity."

- **Create a Supportive Environment:** Foster a family culture that values teamwork and mutual support rather than competition. Encourage siblings to celebrate each other's successes and to support one another through challenges.

- **Communicate Openly:** Talk openly with your children about their feelings and experiences. Validate their emotions and reassure them that they are valued for who they are, not how they compare to their siblings.

- **Be Mindful of Your Language:** Be conscious of the language you use and the potential impact of your words. Avoid making statements that compare your children, and instead focus on addressing each child's needs and achievements individually.

By avoiding negative sibling comparisons and focusing on celebrating each child's unique qualities, you can foster a more supportive and loving family environment. Recognizing the individuality of each child helps to build their self-esteem and strengthens sibling relationships. Remember, the goal is to help each child, regardless of their age, thrive in their own way, creating a harmonious and nurturing family dynamic.

Neglecting Self-Care

As parents, we tend to put our kids' needs before our own. It feels right, doesn't it? But here's the thing—if we neglect our own needs, we end up stressed, burned out, and not as effective as we'd like to be. Taking care of ourselves physically, emotionally, and mentally isn't just important; it's essential. Whether it's reading a book, going for a walk, or catching up with friends, finding activities that recharge you is key. When you're well-rested and happy, you're in a much better place to give your children the love and support they need.

The Importance of Self-Care

Neglecting self-care doesn't just affect us as individuals; it ripples out to the entire family. Think about it: when we're worn out, how can we possibly be at our best for our kids? Taking care of ourselves helps keep the family dynamic healthy and balanced.

Let's start with physical well-being. Regular exercise, enough sleep, and eating right are the basics. When we're physically healthy, we have more energy to engage with our families and handle the day-to-day hustle.

Then there's emotional health. Finding time to relax and unwind helps manage stress and prevents burnout. It allows us to handle conflicts and challenges with a clearer, calmer mind, creating a more harmonious home environment.

Mental resilience is equally important. Engaging in hobbies, learning new skills, or simply enjoying some quiet time can do wonders for our mental state. This mental strength is crucial for making sound decisions and staying patient and supportive, especially during tough times with our kids.

Practical Self-Care Strategies

So, how do we actually take care of ourselves amidst all the chaos of parenting? Here are some practical strategies:

- **Prioritize Your Health**: Make exercise a regular part of your routine, even if it's just a daily walk. Ensure you get enough sleep each night and eat balanced, nutritious meals.

- **Make Time for Yourself**: Set aside time each day for an activity you enjoy, whether it's reading, gardening, or a creative hobby. Practices like mindfulness or meditation can also help manage stress and improve mental clarity.

- **Maintain Social Connections**: Spend time with friends or loved ones who support and uplift you. Joining a group or community that shares your interests can provide a sense of belonging and social engagement.

- **Set Boundaries**: Learn to say no to additional responsibilities that may overwhelm you. Delegate tasks when possible, and involve your family in household chores to distribute the workload more evenly.

- **Seek Professional Support**: If you're struggling with stress, anxiety, or other emotional challenges, don't hesitate to seek professional support. Counseling or therapy can provide valuable strategies and a safe space to express your feelings.

- **Plan Regular Breaks**: Schedule vacations or short breaks to recharge and spend quality time away from daily routines.

The Benefits of Self-Care

When we prioritize self-care, the benefits extend far beyond ourselves. We become more patient and empathetic, better understanding our children's needs and feelings. A well-rested mind is better equipped to tackle problems creatively and effectively, whether it's managing the household or navigating complex family dynamics.

By practicing self-care, we also set a positive example for our children, teaching them the importance of looking after their own well-being. And, of course, a happier, healthier parent is more present and engaged, strengthening the bond with their children and creating a more loving and supportive family environment.

Self-care isn't a luxury; it's a necessity. By taking care of our physical, emotional, and mental health, we can be more effective, loving, and supportive parents. Remember, you can't pour from an empty cup. Prioritize self-care to ensure you're in the best position to provide for your children's needs and nurture a healthy, happy family life.

Ignoring Emotional Needs

It's easy for parents to get caught up in their children's academic achievements and extracurricular activities. We want our kids to succeed and have every opportunity, but sometimes this focus means we overlook their emotional needs. Ignoring emotional needs is a common parenting mistake, and it can have significant consequences for our children, regardless of their age.

The Mistake of Focusing Solely on Achievements

When we concentrate solely on our children's academic or extracurricular success, we might miss signs that they're struggling emotionally. For instance, we might be thrilled when they get good grades or excel in sports, but we might not notice if they're feeling stressed, anxious, or overwhelmed. This can lead to a situation where our kids feel valued only for their accomplishments, not for who they are as individuals.

Imagine your teenager coming home after a long day. You're eager to hear about their test scores or how they did in their game, but they seem withdrawn and quiet. Instead of diving straight into questions about their achievements, take a moment to ask how they're feeling. They might be dealing with issues that have nothing to do with their performance in school or sports.

The Impact of Ignoring Emotional Needs

Ignoring your child's emotional needs can have long-lasting effects. When children don't feel emotionally supported, they might struggle with low self-esteem, anxiety, or depression. They might also have difficulty forming healthy relationships and managing their emotions effectively.

For example, a child who never hears words of empathy and understanding might grow up feeling that their feelings don't matter. They might become adults who struggle to express their emotions or seek help when they need it. They could also feel immense pressure to always perform well, fearing they won't be loved or valued otherwise.

Practical Ways to Avoid This Mistake

So, how can we avoid the mistake of ignoring our children's emotional needs? Here are a few practical tips:

- **Make Time for Regular Check-Ins**: Ask your kids about their day and really listen to their responses. Sometimes, they just need to know that someone cares enough to ask and listen.

- **Encourage Open Communication**: Let your children know that they can talk to you about anything without fear of judgment. When they do open up, respond with empathy and understanding, even if you don't fully agree with their perspective.

- **Create a Safe and Supportive Environment**: Be mindful of how you react to their emotions. Instead of dismissing or downplaying their feelings, validate them. Say things like, "I understand that you're feeling upset," or "It's okay to feel sad sometimes."

- **Show Them That It's Normal to Feel a Range of Emotions**: Share your own experiences and how you've dealt with similar feelings. This helps them understand that it's okay to be vulnerable and that everyone goes through tough times.

- **Be Patient and Available**: Sometimes, kids need time to process their emotions before they're ready to talk. Let them know you're there for them whenever they're ready.

The Benefits of Addressing Emotional Needs

When we focus on our children's emotional needs, the benefits are profound. They feel more secure and understood, which boosts their self-esteem and resilience. They learn how to navigate their emotions healthily and build stronger relationships.

Supporting their emotional well-being also fosters a deeper connection between you and your child. They'll feel more comfortable coming to you with their problems and joys, knowing that you'll listen and support them.

Recognizing and addressing our children's emotional needs is a vital part of parenting. It's not about being perfect; it's about being aware and making small changes that lead to a healthier, more supportive family dynamic. By focusing on emotional support and validation, we help our children grow into well-rounded, emotionally healthy individuals. So, let's make an effort to be present, listen, and show our kids that their feelings matter.

How Parental Growth Benefits Sons and Daughters

Your journey of growth and improvement as a parent directly impacts your children in profound and positive ways. When you become more aware of your own emotions and mistakes, you model emotional intelligence for your children. They learn to understand and manage their own emotions better, leading to healthier relationships and improved mental health. This awareness not only helps them navigate their feelings but also sets a standard for emotional honesty and vulnerability.

As you work on yourself, the bond you share with your children strengthens. They feel a deeper connection, knowing that you are actively striving to be a better parent. This effort shows them that relationships require work and that you value your connection with them enough to make changes. It creates a sense of security and trust, knowing that you are committed to growth.

Children who see their parents learning from mistakes develop a stronger sense of resilience. They understand that setbacks are a natural part of life and that overcoming challenges is possible with effort and perseverance. This resilience equips them to handle their own difficulties with a positive mindset, seeing mistakes as opportunities to learn rather than failures.

By observing how you acknowledge and correct your mistakes, your children learn valuable decision-making skills. They see the importance of evaluating actions, considering consequences, and making thoughtful choices. This process teaches them critical thinking and the value of reflection, which are essential skills for navigating life's complexities.

Creating an environment where mistakes are viewed as opportunities for growth rather than failures significantly boosts your children's self-esteem. They become more confident in their abilities and less afraid of taking risks. This confidence encourages them to explore their potential and embrace challenges, knowing that making mistakes is a part of learning and growing.

Practical Steps for Recognizing and Improving Mistakes

To start recognizing and improving your parenting mistakes, take time to reflect on your interactions with your children. Consider what went well and what didn't. This self-awareness is the first step toward improvement. Don't hesitate to ask your children for feedback. They might offer valuable insights into how you can improve. Questions like, "How did that make you feel?" or "What can I do better?" can open up productive dialogues and help you understand their perspective.

If you've made a mistake, own up to it and apologize. A sincere apology goes a long way in mending any hurt and showing your commitment to bettering yourself. It teaches your children the importance of accountability and the power of a heartfelt apology.

Parenting doesn't come with a manual, but there are plenty of resources available. Books, articles, parenting workshops, and even counseling can provide new perspectives and strategies. Educating yourself equips you with tools and knowledge to handle different situations more effectively.

Change doesn't happen overnight. Be patient with yourself and your children as you work on improving. Celebrate small victories along the way, recognizing that progress is a journey. Setting realistic goals for your parenting journey can also guide your progress. Whether it's spending more quality time with your children, improving communication, or managing stress better, having clear goals helps you stay focused and motivated.

Recognizing and improving your parenting mistakes is a powerful way to strengthen your relationship with your children and foster a healthier, happier family dynamic. It's a journey of growth that benefits everyone involved. So, take a deep breath, embrace the process, and know that every step you take toward becoming a better parent is a step toward a brighter future for your family.

Highlights of The Chapter

In this chapter, we focus on the importance of acknowledging and correcting parenting mistakes, especially with teenagers and adult children. We cover common pitfalls such as over-scheduling, failing to set boundaries, and comparing siblings. We emphasize the value of admitting errors and how this strengthens the parent-child bond. Additionally, the chapter highlights the benefits of parental growth and self-care, offering practical strategies to build healthier relationships with your children.

Key Points to Take Away

- **Admitting Mistakes Strengthens Bonds**: Recognizing and admitting your parenting mistakes can build trust and deepen your connection with your children. It's crucial for fostering open, honest relationships.

- **Avoid Over-Scheduling**: While providing opportunities is important, over-scheduling can lead to stress and burnout for both you and your children. Balance structured activities with downtime and free play.

- **Set and Respect Boundaries**: Clear boundaries provide structure and security, helping children develop self-discipline and responsibility. Avoid invading their privacy, controlling their social life, or making decisions for them without considering their desires.

- **Avoid Comparing Siblings**: Comparing your children can lead to feelings of inadequacy and sibling rivalry. Celebrate each child's unique achievements and qualities to foster self-esteem and healthier sibling relationships.

- **Prioritize Self-Care**: Taking care of your physical, emotional, and mental health is essential. Regular exercise, sufficient sleep, and engaging in activities you enjoy can help you be a more effective, loving parent.

- **Address Emotional Needs**: Focus on your children's emotional well-being, not just their achievements. Regular check-ins, open communication, and creating a supportive environment help them feel valued and understood.

- **Benefit of Parental Growth**: Your personal growth and improvement as a parent directly benefit your children. It teaches them emotional intelligence, resilience, and critical thinking, while strengthening your bond.

- **Practical Steps for Improvement**: Reflect on your interactions, seek feedback from your children, apologize when necessary, educate yourself, and set realistic goals. Recognize that change takes time and celebrate small victories along the way.

Chapter 6: Prioritizing Your Sons and Daughters

In the whirlwind of daily life, it's easy to get caught up in a cycle of providing material support while neglecting the emotional needs of your children. As parents, we often focus primarily on ensuring our children have what they need physically—things like a safe home, nutritious food, and access to education. While these are undeniably important, they represent just one side of the coin. Equally vital is the need to provide emotional and psychological support, which significantly contributes to a child's overall well-being.

Balancing Material and Emotional Support

Providing for your children's material needs is crucial, but it's equally important to ensure they feel emotionally supported.

This means going beyond just meeting their physical needs and focusing on their emotional and psychological well-being.

Material Support

Let's talk about material support first. This includes providing a safe home, nutritious food, and educational opportunities. These are the foundational elements that allow your children to grow and thrive. Ensuring they have these necessities is a fundamental part of parenting. It's like giving them the tools they need to build a solid life.

Emotional Support

But here's where it gets deeper—emotional support. This involves being present, listening, and showing empathy. It's about creating a safe space where your children feel heard and understood. When you're emotionally available, it helps them develop a strong sense of self-worth and confidence. It's not just about being there physically but truly engaging with their feelings and experiences. Emotional support means you are there to guide them through their struggles, help them navigate their feelings, and provide the kind of love and attention that makes them feel valued and understood.

Making Them Feel Valued and Understood

One of the greatest gifts you can give your children is the feeling that they are valued and understood. This involves active listening and validating their feelings. Now, let's delve deeper into the quality of time spent together with your children.

Quality Time

Spending quality time together doesn't have to involve elaborate plans. Simple activities like playing a game, cooking a meal, or going for a walk can create meaningful connections. These moments are opportunities to bond and show your children that they are a priority in your life. It's about making memories and sharing experiences that matter.

When you give your children your undivided attention, you're telling them they matter to you, which can really boost their self-esteem and sense of worth. Imagine a lazy Sunday afternoon spent baking cookies together. It's not just about the cookies; it's about the laughter, the little conversations, and the mess you make along the way. Or think about those walks in the park. These walks can be a great time for your kids to open up about their day, share their thoughts, and just feel heard without any distractions.

Quality time helps build trust and strengthen your bond with your kids. It's during these moments that they feel most comfortable sharing their thoughts and feelings, knowing that you're really listening. This deepens your connection and helps you understand them better, making it easier to support them through whatever they're facing.

In today's busy world, finding time can be tough. But it's so important to prioritize these moments. Even short, regular interactions can have a big impact. It's not about the quantity of time but the quality of the interactions. Sometimes, just five minutes of undistracted, engaged time can be more valuable than hours spent in the same room without really connecting.

The Role of Consistent Parental Support Through Adulthood

Parental support shouldn't end when your children reach adulthood. In fact, consistent support during this stage is crucial as they navigate new challenges and transitions.

As your children step into adulthood, they face a myriad of decisions and obstacles, from choosing a career path to managing finances and relationships. Offering guidance and advice can provide them with the support they need to make informed choices. However, it's essential to balance this with respecting their autonomy and encouraging independence. Think of it like this: your role shifts from being the captain of the ship to being the lighthouse. You're there to provide light and guidance, but they're the ones steering their own course.

Life's challenges don't disappear after adolescence; they merely change. Your adult children might face job stress, relationship issues, or health concerns. Being emotionally available means being there to listen and offer support without judgment. It's about maintaining that safe space where they know they can come to you with anything. This can be as simple as checking in regularly, being a sympathetic ear, or offering words of encouragement. Sometimes, just knowing that you're there and that you care can make a world of difference. It's important to validate their feelings and remind them that it's okay to feel overwhelmed sometimes.

Celebrating your children's achievements and milestones, no matter how small, is incredibly important. These celebrations reinforce that you are proud of them and invested in their happiness and success. Whether it's landing a new job, reaching a personal goal, or just getting through a tough week, showing your pride and joy in their accomplishments matters. Small gestures can go a long way. Sending a congratulatory message, taking them out for a celebratory meal, or even just expressing your pride verbally can boost their confidence and motivate them to keep striving for their goals.

To support your adult children effectively, stay connected through regular communication. Whether it's through phone calls, texts, or video chats, staying in touch helps maintain a strong relationship. Offer help with things like moving, fixing things around the house, or babysitting grandchildren, but avoid being overbearing. Encourage their independence by supporting their decisions, even if you don't always agree with them, and respect their privacy and space. Acknowledge their achievements and milestones, reinforcing that you're invested in their success and happiness.

Developmental Stages

Children's needs evolve as they grow, and so should your approach to providing support. Let's chat about how to tailor your support at different stages:

Infancy and Early Childhood

This stage is all about creating a safe, nurturing environment. Think of it like building the foundation of a house. You want it to be solid and secure. Physical affection is key here—lots of cuddles, kisses, and holding. Babies thrive on touch and feel loved when they're physically close to you. Consistent routines are your best friend. They help your little one know what to expect, which is super comforting for them. So, regular feeding times, nap times, and bedtime routines are golden.

Responsive interactions are also crucial. When your baby coos or cries, respond to them. It might seem simple, but every time you react to their sounds and gestures, you're teaching them that communication works and that they are important. It's like having a conversation even before they can talk.

Middle Childhood

When they hit middle childhood, it's all about encouraging exploration and learning. This is the age where their curiosity really kicks in. Support their interests—whether it's dinosaurs, space, or art. Dive into these topics with them. Get books, watch documentaries, and maybe even take trips to museums or science centers.

Schoolwork starts to play a big role now. Helping them with homework and projects shows you care about their education. But don't just focus on academics. Foster their social skills through playdates and group activities. Team sports, dance classes, or art groups can be great for this. They learn to share, cooperate, and develop empathy.

Adolescence

Ah, the teenage years—a whole new ballgame. Adolescence is when emotions get complex and independence becomes a big deal. Be available to discuss their feelings and the challenges they face. This might mean late-night talks or being a sounding board when they're stressed about school or friendships.

Respecting their need for independence is crucial. They're figuring out who they are, and part of that involves making their own decisions. Of course, they still need guidance, but it's a balancing act. Offer advice, but let them take the lead when possible. Think of yourself as a coach rather than a manager.

Young Adulthood

When your kids step into young adulthood, your role shifts again. Now, you're more of an advisor. They're navigating big decisions—careers, relationships, finances. Offer your advice when they ask for it. Share your experiences, but make sure to respect their autonomy. It's like being a lighthouse—you're there to guide them, but they're the ones steering the ship.

Being emotionally supportive remains important. Life doesn't get easier just because they're older. Regular check-ins, a sympathetic ear, and words of encouragement can make a huge difference. Celebrate their achievements, no matter how small. Whether it's landing a new job or simply surviving a tough week, your pride and joy in their accomplishments matter.

Encourage their independence by supporting their decisions and respecting their privacy and space. They need to know you trust them to handle their own lives while still feeling that you're there for them.

Adulthood

Even when your kids are fully grown, your role as a parent doesn't just stop. It evolves. Your children might have their own families, careers, and homes, but your support remains invaluable.

Continued Emotional Support: Even adults need to know they have someone to turn to. Life's challenges don't disappear—they just change. Regular calls, visits, and messages of encouragement can help maintain a strong emotional bond.

Guidance When Needed: They might not ask for advice as often, but knowing you're there to offer it when they need it can be a great comfort. Share your life experiences and wisdom without imposing. Respect their choices and their need to carve out their own paths.

Celebrate Their Milestones: Just as when they were younger, celebrating their achievements is important. Be it a promotion, a new home, or personal milestones, showing your pride and joy reinforces their sense of accomplishment and confidence.

Respect Their Independence: This is crucial. Support them but let them lead their lives independently. Sometimes, this might mean holding back your advice unless asked and giving them space to handle things in their own way.

Be There in Tough Times: Life can be tough at any age. Your adult children will still face setbacks and hardships. Whether it's job loss, relationship issues, or personal struggles, being a steady source of support can be incredibly comforting.

So, there you have it—supporting your children through different stages is all about adapting your approach to meet their evolving needs. It's a journey, and as long as you're there with love, understanding, and a willingness to adjust, you're doing great.

Highlights of The Chapter

In Chapter 6, we emphasize the importance of balancing material and emotional support for your children. While providing physical necessities is crucial, equally important is attending to their emotional and psychological well-being. We discuss how to make your children feel valued and understood through quality time and consistent parental support, even into adulthood. This chapter highlights the need for tailored support at different developmental stages and offers practical strategies to prioritize your children's overall well-being.

Key Points to Take Away

- **Balancing Material and Emotional Support**: Ensure that while providing for your children's physical needs, you also prioritize their emotional and psychological well-being. Both aspects are crucial for their overall development.

- **Quality Time**: Spend meaningful time with your children through simple activities like cooking, walking, or playing games. These moments help build trust, boost their self-esteem, and deepen your connection.

- **Consistent Support Through Adulthood**: Continue offering guidance and emotional support as your children transition into adulthood. Respect their autonomy while being available to listen and provide advice when needed.

- **Making Them Feel Valued**: Show your children that they are important by actively listening and validating their feelings. This helps them develop a strong sense of self-worth and confidence.

- **Support at Different Developmental Stages**:

  - **Infancy and Early Childhood**: Focus on physical affection, consistent routines, and responsive interactions.

  - **Middle Childhood**: Encourage exploration and learning, support their interests, and help with schoolwork.

  - **Adolescence**: Be available for emotional support, respect their need for independence, and offer guidance.

  - **Young Adulthood**: Act as an advisor, celebrate their achievements, and encourage their independence.

  - **Adulthood**: Provide continued emotional support, offer guidance when asked, celebrate milestones, and respect their independence.

- **Parental Role Evolution**: Understand that your role as a parent evolves as your children grow. From being a provider and protector in early years to a guide and advisor in adulthood, adapt your support to meet their changing needs.

Chapter 7: Conflict Resolution Strategies

Let's take a moment to be honest – no matter how strong your relationship is with your children, conflicts are bound to arise from time to time. It's completely normal and happens in every family. You might find yourself in a heated argument over curfew, feeling misunderstood about your advice, or clashing over different values and life choices. These moments can be tough, leaving you feeling frustrated or even questioning your parenting. But here's the thing – it's not about eliminating conflicts altogether, which is nearly impossible. Instead, it's about learning how to handle them effectively and compassionately. By understanding where these conflicts come from, we can turn challenging moments into opportunities for growth and deeper connection. So, let's explore some common sources of conflict and discover how to navigate them with empathy and understanding.

Differences in Expectations: Imagine this: you think your child should help out more around the house, but they're juggling school, friends, and maybe even a part-time job. Your expectations clash with theirs, and suddenly, conflict arises. It's not just about chores; it's about the larger issue of what each of you expects from the other. Parents often have standards based on their own experiences and beliefs, while children, particularly teens, are trying to manage multiple pressures and might have different priorities. These differing expectations can lead to frustration on both sides, with parents feeling their kids are not meeting their standards, and kids feeling overwhelmed or misunderstood.

Generational Gaps: The generation gap is more than just about you not understanding their obsession with the latest social media app or them rolling their eyes at your old-school preferences. It's about deeper differences in values, experiences, and worldviews. Think about it: you grew up in a different time, with different societal norms and challenges. Your values were shaped by those experiences, and they naturally differ from those of your children, who are growing up in a rapidly changing world. These differences can cause friction, as it might seem like you're speaking entirely different languages, leading to misunderstandings and miscommunications.

Autonomy and Independence: As children grow, they crave more independence. This is a natural part of their development, but it can be hard for parents to adjust. You've spent years guiding and protecting them, and suddenly they want to make their own decisions and carve out their own space. This desire for autonomy can feel like a rejection or a challenge to your authority, leading to power struggles. From the child's perspective, it's about asserting their individuality and gaining confidence in their ability to manage their own lives. These growing pains can be difficult for both sides, often resulting in conflicts over boundaries and freedoms.

Communication Styles: Communication is key in any relationship, but everyone has their own way of expressing themselves. Maybe you're the type who likes to talk things out, while your child is more reserved or prefers to express themselves through actions rather than words. These different styles can lead to misunderstandings. For example, a parent's well-intentioned advice might come across as criticism, or a child's silence might be misinterpreted as defiance or indifference. These mismatched communication styles can create a sense of disconnect, making it hard to understand each other's perspectives and intentions.

Life Transitions: Life is full of changes, and each major transition brings its own set of stresses and potential conflicts. Whether it's starting high school, moving out for college, landing that first job, or getting married, these significant changes can shake up the dynamics of your relationship. These transitions often come with new responsibilities and expectations, which can be stressful. Parents might struggle to let go or adapt to their child's growing independence, while children might feel the pressure to meet new expectations and navigate their changing roles. This period of adjustment can be fraught with misunderstandings and disagreements as both sides try to find their new normal.

By understanding these common sources of conflict, you can approach disagreements with more empathy and patience. It's not about avoiding conflict altogether but about navigating it in a way that strengthens your relationship with your children. Remember, it's okay to have these bumps along the way – they can lead to deeper understanding and a stronger bond.

Navigating Disagreements: Beyond Communication

Conflicts with your children are inevitable, but handling them effectively can strengthen your relationship and foster mutual understanding. Here's a straightforward, five-step guide to navigating disagreements constructively:

Step 1: Emotional Regulation

Pause and Reflect:

- When a conflict arises, take a deep breath and count to ten before responding. This short pause helps you calm down and think more clearly.

- Encourage your child to do the same. Suggest taking a few minutes apart to gather thoughts before continuing the conversation.

Practice Mindfulness:

- Incorporate mindfulness techniques like deep breathing or guided imagery. For example, close your eyes and imagine a calm place, then return to the discussion with a clearer mind.

- Teach these techniques to your child so they can use them when feeling overwhelmed.

Step 2: Setting Boundaries

Establish Clear Limits:

- Agree on ground rules for how to handle disagreements. For instance, no shouting, name-calling, or interrupting.

- Write these rules down and keep them in a visible place, like on the fridge, to remind everyone of the agreed-upon boundaries.

Respect Personal Space:

- If a conflict is escalating, agree to take a "time-out" and come back to the discussion after a set time (e.g., 15 minutes).

- Use this break to cool off and think about the issue more objectively.

Step 3: Problem-Solving Approach

Identify the Issue:

- Clearly state what the disagreement is about. For example, "We are arguing about curfew times."

- Encourage your child to articulate their perspective. This ensures both sides understand what the conflict is really about.

Brainstorm Solutions Together:

- Sit down with your child and list possible solutions without judging them. Let each person suggest ideas.

- Evaluate the pros and cons of each idea together and choose the one that works best for both of you.

Step 4: Mediation and Third-Party Involvement

Seek External Help:

- If conflicts are recurring and unresolved, consider involving a family counselor or mediator. They can provide an unbiased perspective and help facilitate constructive conversations.

- Don't wait until things get out of hand. Seeking help early can prevent conflicts from escalating.

Regular Family Meetings:

- Schedule regular family meetings to discuss any ongoing issues in a structured setting. This proactive approach helps address problems before they become major conflicts.

- Use these meetings to check in on everyone's feelings and discuss any new concerns or updates.

Step 5: Conflict De-escalation Techniques

Agree to Disagree:

- Recognize that it's okay not to agree on everything. Sometimes, acknowledging different viewpoints and agreeing to disagree can be a resolution in itself.

- This can reduce tension and show respect for each other's opinions.

Focus on Resolution, Not Winning:

- Shift the goal from winning the argument to finding a solution. Emphasize that the priority is resolving the issue in a way that maintains a positive relationship.

- Use phrases like "Let's find a solution that works for both of us" instead of "You need to see things my way."

Techniques for Finding Common Ground

Identify Shared Goals:

- Discuss and agree on common objectives, such as maintaining a peaceful home or ensuring everyone's needs are met.

- Write these goals down and refer to them when conflicts arise to remind everyone of the bigger picture.

Compromise:

- Be willing to give and take. For example, if your child wants a later curfew and you're concerned about safety, agree on a compromise like a slightly later curfew with regular check-ins.

- This shows that you value their perspective and are willing to meet halfway.

Problem-Solving Together:

- Approach conflicts as a team. Sit down and brainstorm solutions together, then evaluate and choose the best option.

- This fosters a sense of partnership and encourages your child to be invested in the resolution.

Respect Differences:

- Acknowledge that having different opinions is okay. Show respect for your child's viewpoint even if you don't agree with it.

- This mutual respect can help you find a middle ground

and make future conflicts easier to navigate.

Stay Positive:

- Highlight the positives in your relationship and express gratitude for each other's efforts.

- Regularly acknowledge the things your child does well and the positive aspects of your relationship. This can shift the focus from conflict to cooperation.

By following these steps, you can navigate conflicts with your children in a way that strengthens your relationship and fosters a deeper understanding and connection. Remember, it's not about avoiding conflicts but handling them in a way that promotes growth and harmony.

Techniques for Finding Common Ground

Finding common ground with your children during conflicts is crucial for resolving issues and maintaining a healthy relationship. Here are five practical steps to help you navigate disagreements and find solutions that work for both of you:

Step 1: Identify Shared Goals

Discuss and Agree on Common Objectives:

- Start by discussing and agreeing on shared goals. These could include maintaining a peaceful home, ensuring everyone's needs are met, or supporting each other's personal growth.

- Write these goals down and refer to them during conflicts. This reminds everyone of the bigger picture and helps keep discussions focused on common objectives.

Example:

- Sit down as a family and create a list of shared goals. For instance, "We want a home where everyone feels safe and respected," or "We aim to support each other's ambitions and well-being."

Step 2: Compromise

Be Willing to Give and Take:

- Understand that compromise is key. Be willing to meet halfway to show that you value your child's perspective.

- For example, if your child wants a later curfew and you're concerned about their safety, propose a slightly later curfew with regular check-ins.

Example:

- Discuss the curfew issue openly. "I understand you want more freedom, and I'm concerned about your safety. How about we extend your curfew by an hour if you agree to text me when you're heading home?"

Step 3: Problem-Solving Together

Approach Conflicts as a Team:

- Sit down with your child and brainstorm solutions together. Encourage them to contribute ideas without fear of judgment.

- Evaluate the pros and cons of each idea and choose the one that works best for both of you. This collaborative approach fosters a sense of partnership and encourages your child to be invested in the resolution.

Example:

- For a recurring issue, like messy rooms, brainstorm together: "What can we do to keep your room tidy? Let's list some ideas and see which one feels doable for both of us."

Step 4: Respect Differences

Acknowledge Different Opinions:

- Recognize that it's okay to have different opinions. Show respect for your child's viewpoint even if you don't agree with it.

- This mutual respect can help you find a middle ground and make future conflicts easier to navigate.

Example:

- If your child has a different view on a topic like screen time, acknowledge their perspective: "I see you enjoy spending time online with friends. Let's figure out a balance that works for both of us."

Step 5: Stay Positive

Highlight Positives and Express Gratitude:

- Focus on the positives in your relationship. Regularly acknowledge the things your child does well and the positive aspects of your relationship.

- Expressing gratitude for each other's efforts can shift the focus from conflict to cooperation and foster a more supportive environment.

Example:

- During a calm moment, tell your child, "I really appreciate how you've been helping out with chores lately. It makes a big difference."

By following these steps, you can navigate conflicts with your children in a way that strengthens your relationship and fosters a deeper understanding and connection. Remember, it's not about avoiding conflicts but handling them in a way that promotes growth and harmony.

The Importance of Apologizing and Forgiving

We've already discussed the importance of apologizing and forgiving in previous chapters, but let's delve a bit deeper into why these actions are so crucial for resolving conflicts with your children. Apologizing and forgiving are essential components of conflict resolution because they help heal emotional wounds and restore trust.

When you apologize, it's important to recognize and admit the impact your actions may have had on your child. This shows empathy and responsibility. Imagine telling your child, "I realize that what I said hurt you, and I'm sorry for that." Such words can go a long way in mending the rift. Offering a sincere apology without making excuses is crucial. For instance, saying, "I'm sorry for raising my voice earlier. It wasn't fair to you," demonstrates accountability and a willingness to change. It's also vital to show that you're committed to improving by discussing how you can avoid similar conflicts in the future. This might involve setting new boundaries or changing certain behaviors to prevent misunderstandings.

Forgiving, on the other hand, means letting go of resentment. Holding onto anger and resentment can harm your relationship, so forgiving helps you move forward and heal. It doesn't mean you forget the hurt but rather choose to release the negative emotions tied to it. Try to understand your child's perspective and the reasons behind their actions. This can make it easier to forgive, knowing that everyone makes mistakes and deserves a chance to make amends. Communicating your forgiveness is also essential. Let your child know that you forgive them. This can strengthen your bond and encourage open communication in the future. Saying something like, "I forgive you, and I appreciate that we can talk about this," reinforces your commitment to a healthy relationship.

Conflicts are inevitable in any relationship, but they don't have to be destructive. By understanding the sources of conflict, using tailored strategies for resolution, finding common ground, and practicing apologizing and forgiving, you can resolve conflicts with your children constructively. These strategies not only help in resolving disputes but also strengthen the parent-child relationship, fostering a deeper connection and mutual respect.

Reflect on the last conflict you had with your child. How might these strategies have changed the outcome? Approaching disagreements with empathy, respect, and a willingness to work together can transform conflicts into opportunities for building a stronger, more resilient family bond. What will you try first the next time a disagreement arises?

Highlights of The Chapter

Chapter 7 explores strategies for managing conflicts in family relationships, highlighting their normalcy and potential to strengthen bonds when handled constructively. The chapter emphasizes understanding the root causes of conflicts, which often stem from differences in expectations, generational views, autonomy, and communication styles. It offers practical approaches for conflict resolution, including emotional regulation, setting boundaries, and collaborative problem-solving. Parents are encouraged to handle conflicts with empathy, engage in meaningful dialogue, and seek external help if needed to maintain a healthy family dynamic

Key Points to Take Away

- **Normalcy of Conflicts:** Understand that conflicts are a normal part of parent-child relationships and can be used as opportunities for growth.

- **Empathy and Understanding:** Approach conflicts with empathy, striving to understand the child's perspective and the underlying reasons for their behavior.

- **Emotional Regulation:** Utilize emotional regulation techniques like deep breathing and taking breaks to manage reactions during conflicts.

- **Setting Boundaries:** Establish clear and respectful boundaries for handling disagreements, such as no shouting or interrupting, to maintain a constructive dialogue.

- **Collaborative Problem-Solving:** Engage in problem-solving together, allowing both parent and child to contribute to solutions, fostering mutual respect and understanding.

- **External Support:** Do not hesitate to seek external

help if conflicts become too frequent or severe, using resources like family counseling to provide impartial guidance.

- **Conflict De-escalation:** Focus on de-escalation techniques such as agreeing to disagree and prioritizing resolution over being right, to reduce tension and foster a peaceful resolution.

- **Regular Family Meetings:** Implement regular family meetings to discuss and address ongoing issues in a structured setting, which helps in preventing major conflicts and ensures everyone's concerns are heard and addressed.

Chapter 8: The Rewards of Understanding and Love

As we arrive at the final chapter, it's essential to reflect on the journey we've undertaken—acknowledging our mistakes, learning effective communication strategies, and striving to prioritize our children's emotional well-being. This chapter focuses on the profound rewards that come from fostering a relationship grounded in understanding and love. By building a relationship based on mutual respect and appreciating the long-term benefits of a strong parent-child bond, we can celebrate the journey toward a deeper connection. Here, we put it all together—synthesizing the insights we've explored so far and adding a little more about the power of love and understanding.

Building a Relationship Based on Love and Understanding

At the heart of every strong parent-child relationship is love. This love is not just about providing for your children's needs but about showing them every day that they are valued and cherished. Love is demonstrated through actions and attitudes that convey understanding, empathy, and respect. When you understand your child's needs, thoughts, and feelings, you express a profound form of love that strengthens your bond.

Love in a parent-child relationship isn't static; it's an ongoing, evolving experience that grows deeper over time. It's shown through the big gestures and the small, everyday acts. It's there in the hugs and kisses, the words of encouragement, and the listening ear you offer after a tough day. Love is also in the boundaries you set and the guidance you provide, which show your children that you care about their well-being and their future.

Understanding is a dynamic process that evolves over time. As your children grow, their needs, perspectives, and challenges change. Being attuned to these changes and responding with empathy and support demonstrates ongoing love and commitment. This continuous adaptation is crucial in fostering a resilient and supportive relationship.

When they're young, understanding your children might mean knowing when they need a nap versus a snack, or recognizing when they're scared and need reassurance. As they get older, it involves deeper emotional insight—understanding the pressures they face at school, the complexities of their social lives, and their evolving dreams and fears. It's about being there for the important conversations and the silent companionship.

As your children grow into teenagers and then adults, their needs continue to change. They seek independence but still crave your support and validation. Understanding this balance—when to step in and when to step back—is key. It's recognizing that sometimes they need space, and other times they need you to be right there beside them, even if they don't explicitly ask for it.

Understanding is also about accepting that your children might not always follow the path you envisioned for them. They have their own dreams, personalities, and ways of seeing the world. Embracing their individuality and supporting their unique journeys is a powerful way to show your love. This kind of understanding requires patience and flexibility, but it pays off by fostering a deep, trusting relationship.

Moreover, understanding and love go hand in hand with mutual respect. When you respect your children's thoughts and feelings, even when they differ from your own, you teach them to respect others and themselves. Respecting their opinions, listening without judgment, and valuing their input in family decisions helps them feel important and heard.

This mutual respect lays the foundation for open communication and strengthens your bond. It helps your children feel safe to express themselves and share their lives with you. They know they can come to you with their triumphs and their troubles without fear of criticism or dismissal.

The Effectiveness of Positive Reinforcement

A key aspect of building a loving and understanding relationship is the use of positive reinforcement. Positive reinforcement involves acknowledging and rewarding desirable behaviors, which encourages children to repeat those actions. This approach is effective because it focuses on strengths and successes rather than shortcomings.

When you praise your child for their efforts, accomplishments, or positive behaviors, you boost their self-esteem and motivation. Simple acknowledgments like "I'm proud of how hard you worked on that project" or "You handled that situation very maturely" can significantly impact their confidence and willingness to strive for improvement.

Positive reinforcement helps children feel valued and recognized, reinforcing the notion that their efforts matter and are appreciated. Over time, this builds a strong foundation of trust and mutual respect, as children learn that their parents notice and celebrate their achievements.

The Poor Performance of Reproofs, Criticism, and Punishment

In contrast, relying heavily on reproofs, criticism, and punishment can be detrimental to building a solid long-term relationship with your children. These negative approaches often focus on what children are doing wrong, which can lead to feelings of inadequacy, resentment, and low self-worth.

Criticism and punishment may achieve short-term compliance, but they do not foster genuine understanding or long-lasting positive behavior changes. Instead, they can create a cycle of fear and avoidance, where children might comply out of fear of punishment rather than a true understanding of why their behavior needs to change.

Reproofs and criticism can damage the parent-child relationship by eroding trust and open communication. Children who feel constantly criticized are less likely to share their thoughts and feelings, fearing judgment and disapproval. This can lead to a breakdown in communication and a weaker emotional bond.

Constructive Ways to Show Disappointment

Expressing disappointment constructively is essential for maintaining a child's self-esteem while encouraging better behavior. This approach focuses on specific actions rather than attacking a child's character, helping them understand that while their actions might need improvement, their worth as individuals remains unchanged. These principles apply not only to young children but also to adult children, who continue to benefit from respectful and supportive interactions with their parents.

Behavior-Focused Feedback

Instead of making character-based statements like "You're always lazy," a more constructive approach is to address the specific behavior: "I noticed you didn't finish your homework. Can we talk about what happened and find a solution?" This method clarifies that the concern lies with the action, not the child's inherent qualities. For adult children, this might translate to, "I noticed you haven't been in touch much lately. Is everything okay? Can we find a way to stay more connected?" It encourages reflection on actions and understanding of consequences without feeling attacked or devalued.

Encouraging Problem-Solving

Engaging children, regardless of age, in finding solutions fosters a sense of responsibility and collaboration. For instance, after addressing the unfinished homework with a younger child, a parent might ask, "What do you think could help you complete your assignments on time?" With an adult child, this approach could involve, "I've noticed you seem stressed about work. What do you think would help you manage it better?" This dialogue shows that their input is valued, promoting respect and accountability.

Empathy and Support

Showing empathy is crucial when expressing disappointment. Acknowledge the child's feelings and challenges: "I understand that you might find this subject difficult. Let's figure out a way to make it easier together." For an adult child, this might be, "I know you've got a lot on your plate right now. How can I support you during this tough time?" This approach shows solidarity and willingness to support through difficulties rather than just highlighting failures.

Setting Clear Expectations

Clear and consistent expectations can prevent many issues from arising. When children, young or adult, know what is expected of them and the reasons behind these expectations, they are more likely to meet them. For younger children, it might be,

"We've agreed that finishing homework before playing games is important. Let's talk about how we can stick to this plan." For adult children, it might be, "I know we both have busy lives, but let's try to set aside some time each week to catch up and spend quality time together."

Positive Reinforcement with Constructive Feedback

Balance is key. While it's important to address issues, it's equally vital to acknowledge positive efforts. When combining constructive criticism with positive reinforcement, children, irrespective of age, understand that their efforts are noticed and appreciated, even if the outcome isn't perfect. For a young child: "I'm proud of how you started your homework on your own. Let's figure out how we can make sure it gets completed next time." For an adult child: "I really appreciate how you've been making an effort to visit more often. Let's keep working on staying connected even when life gets busy."

Modeling Desired Behaviors

Parents can model how to handle disappointment and setbacks constructively. Demonstrating calm and thoughtful responses to personal challenges teaches children, both young and adult, how to react similarly. When parents show that it's possible to address problems without resorting to harsh criticism or punishment, children learn to emulate these behaviors in their own lives. For adult children, witnessing parents navigate their own setbacks with resilience and a problem-solving attitude can be particularly impactful.

By focusing on these constructive ways to show disappointment, parents can help their children learn from mistakes and grow without damaging their self-esteem. This approach reinforces the principles of love, understanding, and mutual respect, laying the foundation for a strong, trusting parent-child relationship that evolves positively throughout life.

The Long-Term Benefits of a Strong Parent-Child Bond

The rewards of building a relationship based on love and understanding are profound and long-lasting. A strong parent-child bond contributes significantly to emotional well-being, social development, and even academic and career success.

When a relationship is grounded in love and understanding, it provides a secure base from which children can explore the world. They develop strong self-esteem and emotional resilience, knowing they are loved and valued for who they are. This emotional security helps them navigate life's ups and downs with confidence.

Children who grow up in an environment of love and understanding learn essential social skills. They develop empathy, effective communication, and healthy ways to resolve conflicts. These skills are crucial for forming and maintaining positive relationships throughout their lives.

Supportive parental relationships also contribute to better academic and career outcomes. When children feel emotionally supported, they are more motivated and confident in their abilities. They are likely to pursue their goals with determination, knowing they have a solid support system behind them.

The journey of parenting is filled with challenges and rewards. Celebrating the milestones and acknowledging the growth in your relationship with your children reinforces the bond you share. Reflect on the progress you've made and the understanding you've cultivated. These moments of reflection and celebration are not just about the past but also about looking forward to a future filled with continued growth and connection.

Parenting is an evolving process that demands love, understanding, and continual adaptation. The rewards of building a relationship based on these principles are immeasurable. By focusing on mutual respect and emotional support, you create a strong, lasting bond with your children that enriches both your lives. Celebrate the journey, cherish the moments of connection, and look forward to the future with hope and commitment. The effort you put into understanding and loving your children lays the foundation for a relationship that stands the test of time, providing a source of strength, joy, and fulfillment for years to come.

Highlights of The Chapter

In this last chapter, we've seen the profound benefits of nurturing a relationship based on love and understanding between parents and children. Together, we've recognized the need for empathy and adaptation as children grow, understanding how daily expressions of love reinforce their value. We've explored the emotional, social, and academic advantages of this approach, championed positive reinforcement over criticism, and emphasized constructive feedback and problem-solving. Ultimately, we've affirmed that a strong, respectful parent-child bond is crucial for enduring familial harmony and individual growth.

Key Points to Take Away

- **Love as a Daily Practice:** Show love through actions and attitudes that convey empathy, understanding, and respect.

- **Evolving Understanding:** Stay attuned to the changing needs and challenges of your children as they grow, adjusting your support accordingly.

- **Benefits of a Strong Bond:** A robust parent-child relationship enhances emotional security, social competence, and academic and career success.

- **Positive vs. Negative Reinforcement:** Emphasize positive reinforcement to encourage desirable behaviors, while minimizing criticism and punishment that can erode self-esteem.

- **Constructive Disappointment:** Express disappointment constructively, focusing on specific behaviors rather than personal character, to maintain self-esteem and encourage improvement.

- **Engagement in Problem-Solving:** Involve children in finding solutions to encourage responsibility and collaborative problem-solving.

- **Mutual Respect:** Foster open communication and respect by valuing your children's thoughts and feelings, even when they differ from your own.

- **Celebration of Progress:** Regularly reflect on and celebrate the growth and understanding achieved in your relationship, looking forward to continued connection and support.

Conclusion

As we reach the end of this journey, let's take a moment to reflect on the practical insights we've gained and the hopeful messages we've shared. Throughout this book, we've explored the importance of truly understanding our children, breaking the cycle of misunderstanding, and fostering deeper, more empathetic relationships.

First and foremost, we've learned that acknowledging our own experiences of being misunderstood is the first step toward breaking the cycle. By reflecting on our youth and recognizing that we don't know everything about our children, we open ourselves up to genuine connection.

We've discussed the often unconscious reasons why people have children and how understanding these motivations can shed light on our parenting styles. Recognizing these underlying factors helps us approach parenting with greater awareness and intention.

We've also tackled the issue of parental expectations. It's crucial to avoid placing unrealistic burdens on our children, such as expecting them to care for us in old age. Instead, we should focus on supporting their individual growth and happiness.

Mindful parenting has been a central theme. We've learned to observe and talk to our children beyond surface-level questions, valuing their true feelings and creating a safe space for them to express themselves. This approach builds trust and fosters a deeper understanding.

Communication is key. We've practiced how to really listen to our children, avoiding judgments based solely on their achievements and encouraging open dialogue. These techniques help build a foundation of trust and mutual respect.

In our tech-driven world, we've recognized the importance of addressing technological escapism. By understanding why children turn to screens and helping them find balance, we can foster real-life connections that are essential for their development.

We've acknowledged that every parent makes mistakes. Recognizing and improving on these mistakes is vital. By learning from our errors and growing as parents, we can strengthen our bond with our children.

Prioritizing our children goes beyond providing for them materially. Emotional support is equally important. We've explored how to make our children feel valued and understood, offering consistent support throughout their lives.

Building a relationship based on mutual respect leads to lasting benefits, enriching both our lives and our children's. This journey isn't always easy, but the rewards—a stronger, deeper connection—are immeasurable.

Practical Steps to Strengthen Your Parent-Child Relationship

Reflect on Your Own Childhood: Take some time to think about your own experiences as a child. How were you misunderstood? How can you use these reflections to empathize with your children?

Be Present: Dedicate uninterrupted time to be with your children. Put away distractions and show them that they have your full attention.

Ask Open-Ended Questions: Instead of yes/no questions, ask questions that encourage your children to share their thoughts and feelings. For example, "What was the best part of your day?" or "How do you feel about...?"

Validate Their Feelings: Acknowledge your children's emotions without judgment. Let them know that it's okay to feel whatever they're feeling.

Create a Safe Space: Make your home a place where your children feel safe to express themselves. Let them know they can come to you with anything, without fear of criticism.

Model Healthy Communication: Show your children how to communicate effectively by modeling it yourself. Be open, honest, and respectful in your interactions with them and others.

Balance Technology: Set boundaries for screen time and encourage other activities that foster real-life connections and creativity.

Apologize and Forgive: When you make a mistake, apologize sincerely. Show your children that it's okay to make mistakes and that forgiveness is a part of healthy relationships.

I know we've already talked about these steps, but I wanted to repeat them as my ultimate final words to help cement this information in your mind. These practical steps are not just advice but tools you can revisit time and again. This book is meant to be read and picked up from time to time, not just to beautify your bookshelf.

Moving Forward with Hope and Commitment

Remember, it's never too late to start making positive changes. Embrace the practical insights you've learned here and put them into practice. Reach out to your children with an open heart, ready to listen and understand.

Celebrate the small victories and cherish the moments of connection. Encourage your children to express themselves and show them that their feelings matter. By doing so, you'll create a loving and supportive environment where they can thrive.

As you move forward, stay hopeful and committed to building stronger, more empathetic relationships with your children. The journey may have its challenges, but the rewards are well worth it. A deeper bond, greater understanding, and lasting love await you.

Let's continue this journey together, transforming our relationships with our children, truly understanding them, and building connections based on love and mutual respect. The future is bright, and with dedication and empathy, we can create a lasting impact on our families and beyond.

www.ingramcontent.com/pod-product-compliance
Lightning Source LLC
LaVergne TN
LVHW021824060526
838201LV00058B/3499